The Teacher's Almanac

by

Patricia Woodward

LOWELL HOUSE

LOS ANGELES

CONTEMPORY BOOKS

CHICAGO

Library of Congress Cataloging-in-Publication Data

Woodward, Patricia, 1941-
    The teacher's almanac / by Patricia Woodward.
       p. cm.
    Includes bibliographical references (p.) and index.
    ISBN 1-56565-468-4
    1. Teachers—United States.   2. Teachers—United States—
Social conditions.   3. Teaching—United States.   4. Teacher—
    United States—Conduct of life.   I. Title.
   LB1775.2.W66   1996
    371.1—dc21   96-53318
                                          CIP

Requests for such permissions should be addressed to:
Lowell House
2020 Avenue of the Stars, Suite 300
Los Angeles, CA 90067

Lowell House books can be purchased at special discounts when ordered in bulk for premiums and special sales. Contact Department TC at the address above.

Publisher: Jack Artenstein
Associate Publisher, Lowell House Adult: Bud Sperry
Managing Editor: Maria Magallanes
Text design: Laurie Young

Manufactured in the United States of America
10 9 8 7 6 5 4 3 2 1

To my colleagues—for the ideas they have shared
over the years,
to my students—for their energy and inspiration,
to my family—for their belief and encouragement,

and to Kurt VonderHaar— for his patient
proofreading, excellent editing suggestions, outstanding
computer skills, and loving support.

CONTENTS

Introduction

"In a completely rational society, the best of us
would be teachers and the rest of us would have
to settle for something less."

—Lee Iaccocca

The Teacher's Almanac is designed to give practical tips,
helpful information, words of caution, and useful bits
of insight—perhaps even wisdom—to both the beginning teacher and the seasoned veteran. The professional educator belongs to a sharing profession, one
where we share our expertise, not only with our students, but with each other. When another teacher asks
(or even shows a passing curiosity), we are eager to
share our best ideas, our most carefully thought-out
plans, our favorite techniques, and our most workable
strategies. We cover each other's classes when we can,
and we freely gather any materials that might help a
colleague. We quickly dig out that course syllabus, copy
those daily plans, and lend that creative assignment
that works every time.

Even so, because we are too often isolated from each other—down the hall and around the corner, at the other end of the building, tucked away in a makeshift classroom housed in a temporary structure (usually called an annex)—we sometimes have (or need) information that isn't easily shared. Sometimes we go days or even weeks without really talking to the adults in our buildings, either because we don't see them, or don't have time for more than a hasty hello in passing. Most of us are convinced, or have a strong suspicion, that other people have inside information on subjects we wish we knew more about: how to perform certain tasks more easily, how to conquer the paperwork drudgery, how to teach and still have a family/social life, how to take advantage of travel opportunities and stay abreast of the latest technology and trends. How do they do that?

As professionals, we do have a network, but far too many lack the time and energy to use it (or don't know how to find it). In this book, you will find insights about being professional, ways to develop professionally, ideas for organizing your curriculum and classroom, strategies for balancing your work day, tips on travel opportunities and financial survival, and advice on saving time and energy, plus a section on commonly used terms and a list of important resources for educators. Just turn the page . . .

The Teacher's Almanac

The Professional Teacher

WHAT DOES IT MEAN TO BE PROFESSIONAL?

Originally, the term *professional* was reserved for members of the clergy, doctors, lawyers, and teachers. Today, we hear it applied to anyone who has had specialized training and who pursues an occupation full-time or is gainfully employed in a skilled trade. The term *professional* might be used rather loosely these days; nevertheless, its meaning still has significance. We know that employees are expected to be professional when they are at work; athletes are designated as either amateurs or professionals depending on how they are paid; teachers are perceived as true professionals if they are really dedicated.

We expect a certain standard of behavior from those we deem professional and, yet, many people in education careers neither look nor act professional. Is it the way we dress? Is it how hard we work—whether we punch a clock or set our own hours? Is it the way we talk, the subject matter or the language we use? Is it an attitude, a commitment to our work and our clients? To all of these questions, the answer is yes—to one degree or another.

Whether a teacher wears a suit or is dressed more casually is dictated primarily by the work that is being done. The activities of the day—crawling on the floor with first-graders, or reenacting the Civil War with middle school students—will determine the teacher's clothing, not some arbitrary mandate that insists everyone should wear commonly accepted, appropriate "office attire." Whether a teacher grades papers in the classroom until 5:30 or works in the evening at home is no measure of productivity. Perhaps the most accurate measure of commitment and professionalism is the way we talk to and our attitude toward our clients (our students and their parents).

Teachers have almost always been viewed either as conservative and preservers of tradition, or as radical and inciting society's youth to engage in subversive thought (for example, Socrates, Jesus, and many other famous teachers). In earlier times, a community's moral standards and expectations were clearly stated in the contract teachers signed with the local school board. Teachers were not allowed to patronize bars or to frequent other gathering places of "ill repute"; they were

4

expected to attend religious services regularly; if they were women, they were to remain single. These stipulations were spelled out clearly. Today, however, there are so few specific guidelines that teachers frequently do not know what is expected of them. How should teachers dress, act, talk, or behave? Are there some unspoken guidelines that everyone else is aware of, but nobody talks about until some code has been violated?

Keeping in mind that customs do change, and that some geographic areas are much more tolerant than others, most teachers recognize commonsense guidelines to professionalism in several main categories:

Competence

First, to be a professional is to be very, very good at what you do.

To become a teacher requires a four-year degree at the minimum, with specific training in education techniques and pedagogy, which leads to special certification. Because of this background, teachers are expected to be education "experts." Being a teacher demands by its very nature that we be knowledgeable and that we have high standards for ourselves as well as for our students. That is why we must see ourselves as lifelong learners and continually seek to improve our skills. We won't tolerate second-rate work from our students; why would we allow it from ourselves? We must constantly strive to improve our knowledge, to use the latest technology available, and to hone our communication skills. To send a student home with a notice or letter that has mistakes in it shakes the confidence of parents who expect their child's teacher to know better. Always proofread extra carefully any written communication that leaves your desk! If spelling isn't your forte, ask a colleague to check over your memo. Even easier, with the availability of word-processing programs with spell-check, there is no excuse for misspelled words.

**Commitment and
Appropriate Boundaries**

Second, to be professional requires commitment.

Teaching is not a job to be left at 5:00 in the after-noon and picked up again at 8:00 the next morning. To be professional demands that the teacher do whatever it takes to get the job done. We work whenever, wher-ever, and however we can. We work not just during class time when we're actually with our students, but also whenever we have a chance to think, to plan, to dream, to create: while we're driving the car, working out in the gym, taking a walk, getting our hair cut, doing chores, working on hobbies, or even sleeping. The twenty-four-hour teacher is no myth: even vaca-tions and holidays are usually somehow turned into material for the classroom. Students and their concerns are frequently the first thing teachers think of as they wake up in the morning and the last thing on their minds when they go to sleep at night. More teachers than would admit to it dream about school and even get up in the middle of the night to jot down an idea or work out some problem. We are on call for our stu-dents and their families if they need us, whenever they need us, and that's part of being professional.

This does not mean, however, that teachers have no personal lives or that they have no boundaries. Because of the huge demands made on us (and ones we make on ourselves), teachers must learn to set boundaries. Determine early on how you can best take care of yourself so that you can be there when your students need you. Decide whether you will take phone calls at home and set the hours when you will be available. Determine which activities are within your area of responsibility: it is certainly preferable to say no to a request that asks more of you than you are able to give than to stretch yourself and resent it later. If sponsorship of a student group that is outside your realm of expertise would be better filled by a parent or another community member, say so. Teachers do not have to do it all. Remember: "It takes a whole village to raise a child," and teachers are only one segment—albeit a very important one—of that village.

Draw a professional line between yourself and your students. Many young teachers, especially those starting out, believe that being their students' friend means being their buddy. True, we are our students' friends, in that we care about them, will stand by them, and want what is best for them, but we cannot and should not cross the line and try to be "one of them." If the teacher is not the adult, the one in charge, then who is? Such an attitude only fosters insecurity and distrust in students. This does not mean that we can't have fun with our students, but we should always maintain the attitude and live up to the expectation that the position of teacher requires: being in charge.

Trust and Confidentiality

Third, being a professional teacher carries the responsibility of trust.

A teacher carries a fiduciary responsibility not unlike that of a doctor, lawyer, or priest. The trust that is placed in the teacher is awesome, to say the least. We function *in loco parentis*—we stand in the place of a parent when students are in our charge, whether that's in the classroom, on a field trip, at an extracurricular activity, a school-sponsored function, or a private affair. The trust that is placed in the teacher includes, but is not limited to, responsibility for the students' physical safety, their moral and social behavior, and their psychological and emotional well-being. We must constantly be on guard to protect our students from harm, whether it be from a snowball or an insult being hurled. To create a safe environment is no easy task, nor is it a mere platitude that we can take lightly.

Maintaining confidentiality is one of the most important areas for which teachers are responsible. Teachers should not discuss individual students with anyone unless the setting and purpose are appropriate. Even to discuss students with other teachers in the faculty lounge or over lunch is inappropriate, and if done in public, it becomes unethical. Student names and situations, no matter how innocent, interesting, or controversial, should not be discussed with anyone who is not directly involved with or responsible for those students—period. The best way to handle a direct question or comment is to be noncommittal in your replies, saying little or nothing, without being offensive, and quickly changing the subject. "Now is probably not the best time to talk about ___" usually will handle the situation. Discuss students only with those who have a legitimate concern and only in professional settings.

Student papers and work should never be left where others can see them, nor should work be displayed without the student's permission. Guard the work, grades, and anything else they might not want others to see; keep sensitive materials in a confidential file, put student papers in a folder away from inquisitive eyes, and keep an orderly desk.

Respect for Diversity

Besides protecting student confidentiality, teachers have a professional responsibility to show respect for the religious, political, and social beliefs of all their students. To honor the beliefs of all students, teachers must be keenly aware of the comments we make and the terms we use. We can include all students by using many terms rather than just one: priest, minister, rabbi, religious leader. We must not let our own political or religious attitudes become statements of public record in the classroom. Naturally, our religious and political beliefs will affect the way we respond and react wherever we are, but to openly state such beliefs is inappropriate in the classroom. It violates our purpose and impedes the education of our students, besides showing lack of respect for all youngsters in our charge.

Respect for the ethnic background, sexual orientation, and social customs of our students is also our professional responsibility. As our society becomes more and more diverse, so do our classrooms, and honoring this diversity can sometimes become a challenge for the average teacher. How do we keep up with all the changes and all the expectations our communities have without sacrificing our own standards and beliefs? To foster a climate of acceptance without approving every lifestyle and attitude reflected or represented by the students we teach requires us to walk a very fine line. If we remember, however, that we are working with valuable—yes, precious—individuals whose lives extend far beyond the boundaries of our school yards, we will be able to show that we value the worth of each one. Therefore, it is our professional duty to do or say nothing that would demean or insult any group nor allow an atmosphere that would tolerate slurs of any kind. Such expectations and standards for behavior need to be clearly established early in the year and reinforced by our own actions each day.

Even though the moral and character development of our students is primarily the responsibility of their parents and the community, teachers are expected to set a standard of high morals and good character. Whether we are aware of it or not, our actions, our behavior, and our attitudes often are emulated by the young people in our classes. We *do* influence them, whether we mean to or not. They will follow our example and what we do will have an impact. When we treat our students with respect, they are more likely to treat each other more respectfully. When we are careful not to gossip about other people, they, too, will be more careful about what they say about each other—at least in our classrooms.

When we have a "can-do" attitude about challenges, they are more likely to attempt the difficult. When teachers show acceptance of everyone, students are more likely to be considerate of each other. When we treat everyone fairly, our students will be less likely to deliberately hurt their vulnerable classmates.

Besides being responsible for our students, part of being professional means being responsible to our colleagues. Not only do we have to establish the norms in our own classrooms, but we should uphold the norms of the whole school. What is permissible in one room must not undermine the efforts of the total school environment. In other words, we need to support each other. Our professional responsibility extends beyond the walls of our own classroom to the entire building and beyond our own curriculum to that of the whole school system. Know what the school rules are and enforce them; know what the teacher next to you expects and try to accommodate her; carry your share of the responsibility at extracurricular events, school-sponsored activities, and enrichment opportunities.

Not an easy task, is it? Teaching is not a profession for the weak or the lazy. It is hard work and carries a huge responsibility. For the true professional, however, teaching brings rewards not found in any other field.

HOW TO ORGANIZE YOURSELF—
PROFESSIONALLY AND PERSONALLY

Educators live in a different time zone from the rest of the world. Most people, as soon as the end-of-the-year activities have wound down in December, begin to look ahead to the new year, making New Year's resolutions and starting fresh in January. Teachers, on the other hand, go through this process, not in December and January, but in the middle of the calendar year. For most of us, the old year ends and the new one begins in June. Following is a timetable to serve as a basic guide for planning your professional obligations and for taking care of your personal commitments and responsibilities.

JUNE

Professional:

- Review basic instructional goals, scope and sequence, textbook availability, and materials needed. Make note of revisions in plans and activities you need to make for next year's classes.
- Consider innovative programs to be developed or incorporated into your curriculum.
- Check on resources available through the district or media center.
- Investigate people resources in your community such as collectors, hobbyists, people with unusual or interesting careers to invite as special guests, speakers, or mentors; consider field trips to supplement major curricular objectives.
- Inventory and order supplies for next year.
- Take a class through a staff development program, a university summer class, seminar, or independent study to strengthen your skills and broaden your knowledge (and to meet certification requirements).

Personal:

- Sleep late. Read a novel for fun. Eat slowly.
- Spend time with your family.
- Take a trip—even a short weekend trip will help you unwind.

JULY

Professional:

- Review district policies, insurance coverage, professional certification requirements, and get paperwork in order.
- Continue to think about possible units, activities, and approaches you can use in the upcoming year. This is the time to let your creative juices flow.
- Get to know your community better. Investigate community resources such as museums, libraries, historic sites, businesses, and organizations. Take in some community cultural events.
- Drive through the neighborhood(s) where your students live. Get a sense of where they come from and where they spend their nonschool hours.

Personal:

- Get some exercise: walk, swim, golf, play tennis, or do yard work.
- Do those house repairs and deep cleaning you've been putting off for nine months.
- Really well-organized people do their holiday gift shopping during this time!
- Renew friendships and family ties. Go to reunions and throw a party for your neighbors.

AUGUST

Professional:

- Review your courses and syllabus requirements.
- Compile a list of reference books for each unit.
- Arrange to meet with other teachers in your department or grade level to discuss scope and sequencing, articulation, and potential overlap.
- Plan units, activities, and assignments that can be shared, team taught, and coordinated.
- Plan the year; then the first semester; and finally the first month (or hexter, if you are on a six-week grading system).
- Review student portfolios and cumulative records that are available to you.
- Consider special needs (academic, nonacademic, physical, emotional, social) and religious requirements for observing holidays and participation in class activities (such as flag salute). Use this information to help you plan with all students' needs, strengths, weaknesses, and personal learning styles in mind.
- Get all handouts for the first week of school ready for distribution.
- Set up your room arrangement.
- Double-check on availability of materials, equipment, and supplies.
- Check with your principal or department head for discretionary money to purchase enrichment or supplemental materials.
- Double-check your personal files and papers, receipts, and any applications for special classes you might be considering taking this fall.

Personal:

- Get your annual physical and dental checkup.
- Shop for a new outfit for school. Get a new hairstyle.
- Gear up for the new school year!

SEPTEMBER

Professional:

- Plan a back-to-school activity for students and parents.
- Send out invitations to Back-to-School Night. Students can address them and even write them out; you can add a personal note.
- Consider using daily folders for lesson plans, extra activities, handouts, and forms that are due.
- Make a calendar of your students' birthdays so that you can recognize them on "their day." A special hat, a sign on the chalkboard, a song, or a special treat will bring a smile. A note of caution: Once you remember one, you must remember all birthdays. (Should you miss one, most students are forgiving if you make it up to them somehow—just be sure you do!)

Personal:

- Be sure that your insurance plan is in order.
- Keep exercising. Now is not the time to get so busy that you forget to work out.

OCTOBER

Professional:

- Attend a conference to enhance your professional growth.
- Plan parent conferences. Consider offering to make these home conferences when you can. Many times the teacher can more easily visit a student's home than a parent can leave younger children or get transportation to the school. Your interest and concern will pay huge dividends later.

Personal:

- Start getting ready for the holidays. Do a little gift shopping on the weekends; make plans for parties and holiday meals.
- Dress up for Halloween. Don't forget to play with your kids. (This could appear under the Professional category, too!)

NOVEMBER

Professional:

- Organize a class dinner. Involve parents and families.
- Plan more independent student work to free yourself for one-on-one student/teacher conferences.
- Be sure any requests for special materials or supplies for the holidays have been made.

Personal:

- Plan special time to spend with your family.
- Take a late-afternoon walk with your personal love.
- Watch the sun set from a quiet, secluded spot somewhere (even the back porch, if you have one, will do).

DECEMBER

Professional:

- Check out possible staff development, summer institutes, seminars, and travel opportunities for spring semester and summer.
- Be sure that parents have been contacted about their children's progress. Follow up on students who are having problems meeting standards or developing satisfactorily.
- Plan end-of-semester tests, projects, and changes in schedules; adjust lesson plans to meet the individual needs of your students.

Personal:

- Schedule some time to be alone. You've been giving to others solidly for at least three months now. Do something by yourself for yourself to recharge your own batteries. Go skiing; rent a cabin in the hills; escape to a wildlife retreat; go to the movies on Saturday afternoon—just get away for a couple of hours or, even better, a couple of days.

JANUARY

Professional:

- Start getting ready for second semester.
- Check curriculum guide, materials, and handouts. Plan units for coming months.
- Review individual student progress; make adjustments where necessary.
- Review credits earned for recertification or lane changes (salary increases determined by degrees earned or further education). Determine requirements for professional credentials.
- Check deadlines for applications for any summer programs in which you want to participate.

Personal:

- Gather income tax forms and documents.
- File for an extension by April 15 if you prefer to do your taxes in the summer and you don't anticipate owing additional taxes.
- Schedule an appointment or set aside a block of time soon to work on IRS return.
- Sign up for an exercise program.

FEBRUARY

Professional:

- Contact parents of students who may need extra help. Update student records and portfolios.
- File any applications that are due for summer coursework.

Personal:

- Take a weekend break.
- Go on a spiritual retreat.
- Go to a concert.
- Take part in a community project. It's important for teachers to be involved in the world outside our classroom walls. How can we expect the public to trust us or understand us if they don't know us? Get out there!

MARCH

Professional:

- Review goals and standards; check to be sure all students are making progress toward achieving all proficiencies.
- Double-check summer program application deadlines. File applications that are due.

Personal:

- Start making plans for a vacation—or better yet, take one during spring break.
- Do *not* grade papers over spring break! Plan or plant a garden instead.

APRIL

Professional:

- Start planning for end-of-year activities. Contact parents while there is still time for students to make a final push for improvement.
- Review student portfolios, test scores, and progress toward meeting all academic goals.
- Schedule a performance review with your principal—even if it's not your official evaluation, you could benefit from the current feedback.
- Update your résumé (even if you're not looking for a new job—résumés are often required for all kinds of applications).

Personal:

- Don't forget to file income tax returns if you haven't done so yet.
- Thank a friend.
- Take your daughter, son, nephew, niece, or neighbor kid for an ice cream cone.
- Take a solitary walk in the rain (or the sunshine, if you prefer!).

MAY

Professional:

- Double-check professional growth plan and staff development opportunities.
- Confer with other teachers at your level and in your department to make plans for next year.
- Plan an end-of-year award ceremony.

Personal:

- Remember to get plenty of sleep and exercise; you will need all your energy for end-of-year activities.

JUNE

Professional:

- Plan a great send-off for students as they move to the next grade or level of their educational experience, but never say good-bye. They will be back to see you!
- Prepare a special thank-you for your parent volunteers and others who have helped you during the year.
- Send all end-of-year reports to the appropriate offices, schools, or departments.
- Pack up, label, and carefully store all materials and supplies that can be reused.
- Send any video equipment, computers, or media equipment to be cleaned, repaired, or serviced.
- Collect and send in books to be rebound.
- Inventory and order supplies for next year.

Personal:

- Collapse on the couch and let go and cry if you want. Or go play a round of golf. Whatever you do, remember that stress release is a must for you and you deserve a reward for a job well done.
- Take a big deep breath—it's about to begin again!

What a wonderful world teachers work and live in! Every year we get a fresh start, a new beginning, and another chance to touch a life and enrich our own.

Getting
Organized

When visitors come into the typical classroom and
observe for any length of time, they are almost always
amazed by how much is constantly going on, by the
level of activity the students are engaged in, and by the
number of decisions that teachers have to make. At
first, they may think this is just organized chaos, but
once they get past their initial intimidation, even the
most casual observers come to recognize that the key
word here is "organized." Organization is absolutely
necessary to the success of any teacher, and it begins
weeks—usually months—before the school year begins.

The more organized you can be, the more effective
your teaching will be, and the less stressful your life will
be. This is a job that requires planning, and even though
you will inevitably have to improvise from time to time,

you can't "wing it" very often by simply reacting to each individual crisis, unless you want to be out of control and at the mercy of events. The more planning and thought you can put into the preparation of your classes, the better off both you and your students will be, and the less you will feel like all you do is "put out little brushfires all day long."

Everyone will tell you: **Get organized.** All right. How do you do that?

Begin early. Start off the new year right and then continue as the year progresses. As soon as you get a teaching assignment, start the planning process. If you are a new teacher who is lucky enough to get your contract in the spring, you will have the whole summer to plan. Use it—you'll need it. If you get hired the day before school starts (and that happens more often than we like to admit), you may have to do your planning fast and in a condensed version, but the order will still be the same. If you are a returning teacher, you will have the luxury, we hope, of having a block of time to work on the upcoming year. Again, use it. Take advantage of whatever time you have available for planning. The more time you spend on organizing before school starts, the more time (and energy) you'll have for actually teaching.

ORGANIZING THE CURRICULUM

Plan the curriculum: Let's start with first things first. What are you going to teach?

Assuming that you know your subject matter, and

that the district/state mandates or requirements are clearly stated, the first step in organizing the school year begins not with the daily lesson plan, but with the *course syllabus or outline*. For some teachers the curriculum is predetermined and ready to be implemented, but for others the curriculum will need to be worked out by the individual teacher. If the course curriculum has already been written, you will naturally begin with that to determine general instruction goals and topics, the scope and sequence of skills to be taught, and possible instructional activities. Whether you have complete autonomy or very little flexibility, you will still need to decide where to begin and how to get started.

Plan for the school year: The most efficient way to plan is to look at the big picture. What standards must be met in this course? What skills must be learned this year? Only after you have clearly established what you want the outcome to be can you decide on the materials to be used or the activities and assignments to be offered. Write down the standards, outcomes, and skills to be mastered by your students. Determine the sequence that is most logical and plan out the whole semester; if it is a year-long course, plan both semesters.

Then decide on the standards to be met by each unit. What skills must be addressed and what assignments will best help students achieve them? What do you want your students to know and be able to do as a consequence of this learning experience? Decide what necessary basic concepts must be mastered and then build on those, including a variety of enrichment activities for everyone and challenging opportunities for the

23

more capable and/or motivated. Look at the materials available to you. In all practicality, that's what will dictate much of what you do. We all have to work within limited budgets, and if equipment, materials, supplies, technology, and even books are not available, the best - laid plans will go awry (to broadly paraphrase the Scottish poet).

Look at the materials: What is available to you? What are you going to use to teach? Before the beginning of the school year, take the time to familiarize yourself with the resources in your building, your media center, and in your district main offices. You would be surprised at how many people discover excellent materials sitting on a shelf somewhere, unknown to teachers or forgotten by whoever ordered them. Browse, snoop, dig through file cabinets and in closets. You will find all kinds of materials and resources in your department offices, in your media center and maybe even stored in your own classroom.

Search out the district or main administration office and talk to the resource curriculum specialists for your discipline. Find out what is available in their libraries, on their shelves, and in their files. Most materials are usually available to teachers, but once school starts, most of us don't have time to go looking. Do it before you get too deep in the planning stage. This may sound elementary, my dear, but count your books, check over your equipment, see that it is in good shape, and that students will have access to whatever they will need to meet the requirements for your class. Don't be caught with a great plan and no way to execute it.

Units of study: After you have determined who and what you are going to teach and what you have to teach with, ask yourself what skills build on each other and which ones your students will need to master in order to succeed, and organize the year accordingly by units of study. Sometimes the order will be very natural because learning one skill is dependent upon the mastery of a more basic one first. There will be times, however, when you might have more options because the skills to be mastered are more independent of each other or more discrete. For example, a student will need to know the alphabet before learning to read, but whether a student studies the literary aspects of short stories before poetry may be at the discretion of the teacher.

Once the order of units is determined, you will need to decide how long to spend on each one. This can sometimes be difficult not only for the new teacher, but also for the most experienced educator. Depending upon the complexity of the material to be covered, the abilities of the students, the size of your class, and the types of learning experiences you want your students to have, you can extend or shorten by days or weeks any unit of study. Notice the plural use of *abilities*—your students will probably possess a wide range of abilities even in the most homogeneous grouping. With the trend toward less ability grouping and more inclusion of all kinds of learning needs and styles in one classroom, the range is growing even greater.

First, who are you going to teach? Before you ever see your students you must have them clearly in mind. Although you may not even know their names yet (or if you do have class rolls, you haven't connected a name with a face, let alone a personality), you should have an idea of their level and their educational experience in general. You need to sit down and ask yourself, "What are my students going to need to learn in this class this year?"

Then, keeping in mind the various learning styles your students may have and the types of needs that must be met, determine what activities will best bring about the desired results. Write down the skills, and then list the types of activities or assignments that will be used to teach them. Include a variety of hands-on activities, seat work, group activities, and types of evaluations. You will need to make broad plans at this point; the actual lesson planning for each day will come later.

Assignment calendar: A useful tool at this point is an assignment calendar, which can be used not only as a guide for your daily plans, but as a study guide and accountability tool for students. (See sample on page 28.) It can be done on a monthly basis, or by hexters if you are on the six-weeks grading system. Students, depending upon their age and maturity, appreciate knowing exactly what is going to be expected of them in the coming weeks, parents have a clear picture of what is being studied in your classroom, and absent students can more easily keep up. You need to include due dates, major assignments, performances, tests, and special events, and you might add special notations such as specific materials that might be needed, changes in location, and schedule variations. Even if you don't pass out the assignment calendar to your students, it is an incredibly valuable tool for your own use and accountability. Granted, you will undoubtedly get off schedule, what with all the interruptions and surprises we are blessed with, but with experience you will find that you can plan pretty close to the mark. If you do find that you are behind schedule, simply make the necessary adjustments with your students, asking them to write in the changes wherever necessary, or put out an update from time to time. Whatever you do, don't become a slave to the calendar. Like all good organizational plans, flexibility is crucial to its success.

With the comprehensive long-term planning that you invest in the course syllabus and monthly calendars, making daily lesson plans will be significantly easier. You will have an overview that will provide continuity and structure, that will save you hours of planning time during the year, and you will feel well organized.

Lesson plans: Finally, you are ready to write daily lesson plans. They need to be done on a weekly basis in order to maintain flexibility but still provide adequate planning time. Don't try to come up with a plan on your way to class! Nothing is more unsettling (panic-inducing) than to be wondering what you're going to do in class today. Beginning teachers often ask "old-timers" if they really write down everything. Some do; some don't. My advice is: Write it down. There is no substitute for careful, deliberate planning. Without it, you and your students will flounder, losing precious time that can never be recaptured. Whether you keep your plans in a preprinted planning book, or in a loose-leaf notebook, or on a computer, you will need to know exactly what you and your students will be doing. Whatever

FIGURE 2-1

Assignment Calendar for English

SUNDAY	MONDAY	TUESDAY
31	• Computer lab to begin writing documented essay • Final thesis and out line due **1**	• Organize notecards according to outline • Write essay in computer lab **2**
• Daylight Savings Time set ahead 1 hour **7**	• COMPUTER LAB TO WRITE DOCUMENTED ESSAY ALL THIS WEEK **8**	• All preliminary work will be counted on this hexter's grade **9**
14	• BEGIN POETRY • Take reading locater test • Write response to "What is poetry?" **15**	• MUSIC AS POETRY: Listen to your music. Respond in Poetry Notebook • Work on portfolios **16**
21	• Earth Day • Review terms and concepts required to meet standard for poetry literary terms and techniques **22**	• Reading level test T/W/or Th during 1–2 periods • Read pp. 382–387 Answer both #2 questions in Poetry Notebook **23**
28	• Listen to ballads Review ballad characterisitics **29**	• Analyze "The Ballad of Wm. Sycamore" **30**

APRIL 1996

WEDNESDAY	THURSDAY	FRIDAY	SATURDAY
• We will work in the computer lab April 8-12 **3**	• NO SCHOOL **4**	• Final documented essay will be due April 12 • NO SCHOOL **5**	**6**
• Continue writing essay **10**	• Be sure to check rough draft with Mrs. W **11**	• DOCUMENTED ESSAY DUE • End of 5th hexter **12**	**13**
• Listen to your music! How is this poetry? • Respond in Poetry Notebook **17**	• Listen to your music . . . respond. Be sure to point out poetic qualities in your Poetry Notebook **18**	• Discussion **19**	**20**
• Read pp. 388–389. Write a poem about your own ancestors in your Poetry Notebook. **24**	• Read pp. 390–392. Answer questions 1–5, p. 390. Know the poetry terms on p. 392. **25**	• Discussion **26**	**27**
1	**2**	**3**	**4**

style you use for daily lesson planning, be sure you do it regularly, faithfully, and preferably at the same time each week. Friday afternoons work well; some may leave this duty until Sunday night; just remember, Monday morning over your Cheerios is too late!

ORGANIZING THE CLASSROOM

Once you have your curriculum, materials, and lessons organized, turn your attention to the classroom itself. Create a "user-friendly" atmosphere: posters, plants, lots of color! The classroom isn't just yours, but your students' as well. Make it an inviting place. Most teachers like to spend some time in the room before the first day of school, arranging desks, hanging posters, putting out books, setting out plants, getting the feel of the room where they and their students will be spending the biggest share of their waking hours during the coming school year. The kind of atmosphere you create is a deliberate action on your part—it doesn't just happen. If you want to foster reading and curiosity, you have to plan for it and make it attractive. The classroom management you want to establish will begin with the messages you send your students when you are setting up your room. Where you place your desk (if you use one), where you arrange learning centers, where you keep materials to be checked out, and where you store supplies will all be determined by the kinds of activities in which you want your students to be involved.

Seating arrangements: Whether you use straight rows or clusters of student desks, groups of tables, or a big circle of chairs, the choice will depend upon the kind of learning activities in which your students are going to be engaged. The first day of school, however, may not be the best time to have a relaxed, informal setting for most grade levels. Naturally, kindergartners and junior high students will react differently to a room's arrangement, but the placement of desks or chairs will impact students' behavior no matter their age—so think it through carefully. Teachers should be able to see all students at all times; materials and supplies should be readily available; students should be able to see all presentations; and high-traffic areas such as doorways, pencil sharpeners, waste baskets, and supply cabinets should not be blocked by desks. The physical education teacher and the music teacher will have special requirements to consider, as will other special teachers. Nevertheless, beginning more formally and changing the room's arrangement throughout the year according to the educational demands of your plans and of your students' needs is usually the most effective strategy.

ORGANIZING MATERIALS AND RECORDS

Once you have the room arranged to your satisfaction, you need to spend some time setting up a system for keeping track of everything. Books must be counted and checked out (and back in), equipment must be maintained and accounted for, materials must be ordered (and inventoried), grades must be recorded and standards met, parents must be contacted, and school support personnel (such as counselors, social workers, and school psychiatrists) consulted. The paperwork alone will bury you if you don't have a system. Develop a system for grading, keeping records, and communicating with other education professionals and parents. Whether you use notebooks, computer programs, folders, card files, or any combination of these, you need to have a system that works for you. You may need different systems for different purposes, but figure out a way to stay organized and keep it simple.

Each discipline or grade level has its own requirements as far as specifics that must be accounted for, whether they be classroom art supplies, sheet music, or basketballs, but every teacher must keep records of grades, communicate with parents, and fill out a never-ending stream of forms of one kind or another. Developing a method for dealing with each of these necessities of a teacher's job will make your life much easier.

Grades: Find out what grading system is required by your school district and your individual school, and incorporate those requirements into your system. Talk to the other teachers in your department or grade level and learn what works for them and why. Whether you use a preprinted grade book (which you can usually get from your school's main office), a loose-leaf notebook of your own device, or a computer program, you need to be consistent and up-to-date. Using an objective point system that can be translated into a letter grade is usually more defensible than assigning only a letter grade, which seems to be too subjective. In other words, when students earn points for specific work and know what percentage they must have to get an A for the course, the element of confusion and the possibility of argument are dramatically decreased.

Whatever handwritten record of grades you choose to keep, a good computer program is the best in the long run. Having determined what standards must be met for your class, enter them as categories for the specific assignments that help meet those standards. Not only will you have a record of grades, you will also have a record of what standards have been met and how they were achieved. The computer record is easily corrected and maintained, and at the end of the hexter, quarter, or semester, final grades will already be figured, saving you hours of work when you most need a break! See chapter 3 for more tips on grading systems.

Paperwork: Other ever-present paper demands are the ones made by other professionals. These range from daily attendance rolls, lunch records, athletic eligibility lists, special education student progress reports, and daily progress reports for failing or near-failing students, to special requests from other teachers, counselors, principals, administrators, and frequently, even former students. The best way to handle these reports is immediately. Handle each piece of paper only once, if at all possible. Pick it up, fill it out, turn it in. If that's not feasible, have a specially marked folder for these essential papers and take care of them before they are due. At the end of each day, check the folder to make sure you haven't let something slip by.

Communicating with parents: This is absolutely essential to both your students' success and your own. Frequent and varied contact with parents will benefit everyone, especially the students. Besides keeping parents informed, it encourages their participation and demonstrates to the students that the parent and teacher are working together to help them succeed. Be positive. Send out postcards with short upbeat messages throughout the year. At the beginning of the term, have older students address cards to anyone they would like to have hear a good word about them: parents, grandparents, noncustodial parents, aunts, uncles, whoever. Then write a quick sentence or two whenever the opportunity presents itself. Send home frequent grade reports. These can be computer printouts used to supplement the regular report cards sent out by the school. If you wait until report card time to contact parents, you will have wasted precious time and lost valuable parental support. Parents need to know as soon as possible how their child is performing, and not be surprised when the report card comes home. This goes for the A student as well as for the failing one. Don't overlook the quiet or the high-achieving student, just because you don't see any concerns; their parents want to know how they are doing, just as do the parents of students with obvious problems.

Utilize (or help establish) a twenty-four-hour computerized telephone hot line for grades and attendance. With the aid of modern technology, it is possible for schools to utilize the "anytime info line" approach to communicating with parents. By punching in a student identification number, parents are able to contact the school twenty-four hours a day, keeping themselves informed more easily and regularly than ever before.

Even though the system may not give a specific report on each student, it generally will give enough information so that a parent will know whether a student is attending class, turning in assignments, displaying behavior concerns, passing or failing a course, and whether the parent should contact the teacher. Parents will no longer have to wonder if they have missed a note, or have to wait for their child's report card, or to schedule a parent/teacher conference. Even though standard methods will still be used, the "hot line" can be the instant report that many parents need.

Schedule regular and frequent parent conferences. Nothing can take the place of face-to-face communication. Depending on the grade level, the type and frequency of parent/teacher conferences may vary, but they are nevertheless important to the parents' sense of being involved with their child's education and with that child's success in your classroom.

School Days—

Teaching Tips for Success

BE PREPARED FOR
(AND FROM) THE FIRST DAY

The key phrase here is *be prepared.* It will give you a feeling of confidence like nothing else can do. Your students will pick up on that and consequently have more confidence in you as well.

Equipment and Materials

Be sure that all equipment you will need is checked out and in place. This means going to the media center yourself (or other holding area for special equipment you might need in your particular field) and picking up any overhead projectors, television sets, audio equipment, and computers you will need. Take the time to practice using equipment before the students try it or before you try demonstrating in front of students. A burned-out light bulb can spoil an otherwise excellent lesson in short order. Being prepared means actually having worked through any sequence of steps yourself and knowing that your equipment is ready to use.

Have all materials stocked and ready to use. Think about your own (and your students') needs in the classroom and be sure to have plenty of chalk, staples, glue, tape, special marking pens, transparency markers and sheets, construction paper, computer paper, index cards, and extra pens and pencils, in addition to the required textbooks and supplemental materials you will be using. Lay out or store in a convenient, secure place any materials you will be needing in the next few weeks.

Handouts and Announcements
Be sure that any handouts to be distributed are prepared and double-checked for accuracy. The sooner you can get these run off and ready to hand out, the better off you will be. There will be a run on copying machines at the last minute, and if you can get in the habit of having these materials ready early, you will save yourself many a headache when the copier breaks down or there is a long line ahead of you on the day you desperately need to use it. Before you run off anything, however, have someone else (a colleague, a spouse, a friend) who is a good proofreader go over it for mistakes or omissions. We have a tendency to notice what we want or expect to see, and another person will often pick up the little but crucial error we might have overlooked ourselves.

It is a good idea to have simple, clear explanations of classroom expectations, procedures, and requirements in writing for your students at this time. Remember to include parents in your communication and ask them to reinforce the students' understanding of this important information. You might consider sending home a letter or flyer and asking parents to sign and return it indicating that they have received this information. This document does not have to be so lengthy and detailed that it is overwhelming, but it should include the most basic and necessary information. It may be your first communication with parents, unless you are fortunate enough to be able to meet with them somehow before school starts, and you want to be clear, specific, and informative without being tedious or confusing. (See sample on page 41.)

Any announcements and procedures that you need to review with students during the first few days should be written out so that nothing is forgotten. It is easy to leave out one tiny (yet essential) piece of information, especially if you repeat the same set of instructions to several different classes. Having a written list for yourself (on the board so that everyone can see it is even better) will ensure that you don't forget to tell everyone the same thing—and, believe me, students will be the first ones to say, "You never told us that!"

Preparing the Classroom

Do a final run-through of the room the day before school starts. Start from the hallway in front of the door and look at your room through the students' eyes:

39

- Is the room easily identifiable and approachable?
- Is your name clearly posted on the door and in the front of the room?
- If appropriate, are students' names also clearly posted near the door?
- Does the room look ready for student use?
- Is it clean, orderly, decorated, supplied, friendly, and prepared?
- Are posters and bulletin boards attractive, and learning centers inviting?

Then look for the behind-the-scene necessities:

- Are you familiar with your school manual and district procedures, policies, rules, and regulations?
- Are equipment, furniture, supplies, and materials in place?
- Are there extra desks for late arrivals or transfer students?
- Are the date and plan for the day posted and necessary information in plain view?
- Are the class roster and attendance sheets on your desk?
- Are lesson plans for the first week on your desk?
- Do you have ready all teaching materials for the first day?

FIGURE 3-1
SAMPLE GUIDING PRINCIPLES

Freshman English • Lincoln Jr. High
Mrs. Pat Woodward, Teacher

Welcome back to school! The following "guiding principles" will help you get off on the right foot in Freshman English. Please read them carefully, and share them with your parents.

THE FOLLOWING SUPPLIES WILL BE REQUIRED EVERY DAY:

*a loose-leaf notebook with college-ruled notebook paper
*blue or black ink pen and a #2 pencil
*appropriate textbook

HOMEWORK: Although homework in English class is often necessary, it probably will not be assigned every day. Much of the student's work is accomplished in class, but students will occasionally need additional time outside the classroom. When homework is required, students will be notified either in class or via **the assignment calendar**, which will be handed out every month. **Homework will be counted for a grade.** Frequency and length of assignments will vary but usually **will be noted on the assignment calendar.**

(*Note: All work to be turned in for a grade will be either in #2 pencil, blue or black ink, or typed, according to the teacher's instructions. Papers will be headed with the student's full name, assignment, class and date, beginning on the first line in the upper right-hand corner. Then, skip a line and begin the assignment.*)

LATE WORK: Ten (10) percent—one letter grade—will be taken off the earned grade for each day the work is late, through five (5) days. After five days, work will automatically receive 50% credit. **Late work will not be accepted after the teacher's cutoff date** for the hexter.

ABSENCES: Work missed due to any absence must be made up and may be done so without penalty if completed in a timely fashion. The student must arrange for the due date and the details of the makeup work with the teacher

TARDIES: Students are to be in their seats when the bell rings. An unexcused tardy will result in an automatic detention.

GRADES: Points are accumulated through a variety of assignments during the hexter. They are then converted to a percentage of the total required points to determine the letter or grade for the report card. Grades will be figured cumulatively from the first day of the semester through the end of the semester.

$$90–100\% = A$$
$$80–89\% \ = B$$
$$70–79\% \ = C$$
$$60–69\% \ = D$$

Pat Woodward, Teacher
493-8427 (Home)
484-3073 (School)

Student signature* _____

Parent signature* _____
(or guardian)

*Return with both signatures by September 4, 1996.

FIGURE 3-2

ALTERNATIVE SAMPLE GUIDING PRINCIPLES

Freshman English • Room 114
Mrs. Pat Woodward, Teacher

All students are expected to be:

PUNCTUAL . . . PREPARED . . . POLITE . . . PRODUCTIVE

MATERIALS: Paper, pencil and/or pen (blue or black ink only), a thin, two-division notebook, appropriate texts, assignments, a recommended 3.5-inch floppy disk (to save written work from computer), and appropriate other materials as assigned.

GRADES: Grades will be computed on the total number of accumulated points throughout the semester. The grading scale for **hexter and semester** grades is:

A	90–100%
B	80–89
C	70–79
D	60–69
F	0–59

Late assignments will be reduced by 10% of their grades for each day late.

Late assignments due to excused absences may earn **full credit** if received within one week of the student's return.

Late or missing assignments may be redone once for **80% credit.**

Punctual assignments may be redone once for **full credit.**

CURRICULUM: Topics of study will include, but not be limited to, grammar, usage, and poetry; the novel; vocabulary and spelling skills; the writing process and types of writing; and research. An assignment calendar will be distributed on the first of each month.

STUDENT
SIGNATURE:_____DATE:_____

PARENTS: Please acknowledge your awareness of my expectations, curriculum content, materials needed, etc., by signing below. Please feel free to contact me at school (484-3073) or at home (493-8427) if you have any questions or concerns about my class or your student's progress.
Thank you.

Mrs. Woodward

PARENT
SIGNATURE:_____DATE:_____

FIGURE 3-3
SAMPLE CLASS OUTLINE

Speech • Lincoln Jr. High
Mrs. Woodward, Teacher

SPEECH STANDARDS:

A student who has successfully completed the basic speech course will be able to:

#1. organize a speech

#2. impact an audience

#3. listen respectfully and critically through active listening

#4. demonstrate effective group communication skills

UNITS OF STUDY:

I. Learning about self as member of a group/audience and as a speaker (work on skills in listening and building confidence in presentation)

1. Classmate introduction speech—1st week

2. Group chapter presentations—2nd week

3. Autobiography poster speech—3rd week
    (Standards #1, 2, 3, 4)

II. Organization

1. Outlining—4th week

2. Informative speech—4th and 5th weeks
    (Standards #1, 2, 3)

III. Delivery Skills

1. Visual aids speech—5th week

2. Demonstration speech—6th week

3. Oral interpretation—7th and 8th weeks
    (Standards #1, 2, 3, 4)

IV. Persuasion
1. Speech to convince—9th week
2. Original oratory—10th and 11th weeks
3. Debate—12th and 13th weeks
   (Standards #1, 2, 3, 4)

V. Group Process
1. Discussion—14th and 15th weeks
2. Business meetings/parliamentary procedure—16th week
   (if time allows)
   (Standards #1, 2, 3, 4)

Final speeches—17th and 18th weeks

Classroom Management

After you have planned the year carefully, taken care of the physical aspects of your classroom, and set up a system for paperwork and record keeping, you are ready to take on the challenge of the students themselves. All the efficiency, creativity, well-stocked supply closets, brilliantly written lesson plans, and brightly colored bulletin boards in the world aren't going to teach the students anything unless you can create an environment where every student can learn—and that means classroom management, which basically means *discipline*. Maintaining good student discipline is probably the most challenging aspect of teaching for most teachers, whether they are brand new in the profession or about to retire. How do we maintain order without stifling creativity? How do we teach respect without creating robots? How do we "create a learning atmosphere" without insisting on total silence at all times? How do we maintain authority without being authoritarian?

At the beginning of the school term, training the students is of extreme importance. They need to know what to expect and how to accomplish those expectations. This is meant in the most respectful way, but they are like puppies in that you have to train them quickly and consistently to be self-disciplined; unlike puppies, they will grow to be self-sufficient—which, after all, is the goal of education.

Specific classroom procedures: Train the students in what they are to do when they first come into your room. Be very specific about where and how to sit (take a learning position: feet on the floor, shoulders back,

47

eyes toward the teacher), whether to talk or not, and how to get ready for class to begin. This way, they will begin to focus on the task at hand when they enter the room. These instructions do not have to be given in a heavy-handed way, but students respond better when they know specifically what is expected of them—especially if you can work in a little humor and have fun in the process.

Have supplies and materials in an accessible, convenient place where students can pick up and store these things by themselves. You can minimize the amount of work you have to do by teaching students to take care of their own needs.

Write the day's plans and date in the same place every day, so that students don't have to ask, "What are we gonna do today?" (They will ask anyway, but they won't have to!)

Establish some routine activities to begin the day: board problems to solve, riddles to answer, sentences to correct, daily journal writing, or other warm-up exercises appropriate for your class and students.

Make these opening routines exactly that—routine. When the students know what to expect when they first come into the room, the security of the familiar routine helps them settle in quickly, even when you are not there. This is not to say that every day is exactly the same, but that the beginning routines become established and familiar. Most students need a structured schedule, with an organized setting and consistent responses, in order to feel safe and to perform well. They don't have to be quiet little automatons to achieve this atmosphere of orderliness; they simply need to know that you are in charge, that you have planned for them, and that you have certain expectations of them. Then, the more actively they are involved (the busier they are), the less time they will have for getting into trouble. Again, you don't need to be rigid to accomplish this, but you do need to have some sense of order to be able to achieve a relaxed, spontaneous, free, and happy atmosphere that will provide a healthy learning environment for all your students.

Rewards and reinforcement: All students need attention. If you notice their good behavior and reward it immediately, you will not only be giving them the attention they need and deserve, but you will also be encouraging the behavior you want to see continue. We all know that not calling attention to behavior you don't want to reinforce is usually effective and that reward works better than punishment. Reward doesn't necessarily mean handing out M & M's every time they raise their hands (though most junior high students will leap tall buildings for a Jolly Rancher), but a quick smile, a sincere compliment (sometimes given privately, especially to students who don't want everyone's attention— just yours), or a word of encouragement will go a long way. A private word works well when a student does need to be reprimanded or reminded. It is best done quickly and quietly so that no one else hears. Otherwise, a time-out in an area set aside for this purpose is most effective. Simply ask the student to wait for you there, and then speak to him or her as soon as possible, while the other students are engaged in another activity and you can focus on this one individual.

Establishing rules: Have clear expectations; encourage your students to help you establish the norms for your classroom (about four or five rules everyone agrees upon). Some people have only one rule: "You can do anything as long as it doesn't interfere with anyone else's learning." Or, "Respect yourself and the rights and property of others." For many students, however, more specific guidelines are necessary and appropriate. The extent to which students' management of their own classroom discipline can be successful depends upon the age and maturity of your students, but the more you can involve them in establishing the norms for their classroom behavior, the more personal stake they will have in the rules and, consequently, the more successful they will be. Just don't bombard them with so many rules that keeping track of them is a burden even for you!

Model behavior: As the year progresses, model the behavior you want to see your students exhibit. If you ask them for silence while completing a test, don't stand in the back of the room and talk to someone yourself. If your students are expected to talk quietly, moderate your own tone of voice. If you expect respect from your students, always treat them with respect. If you expect your students to be prepared for class and ready to learn, you had better be prepared and ready to teach. Have the assignment on the board and everything ready to begin before any student comes into the room, even if it means getting to school an hour early.

Promptness: Start the class on time. If you establish early on that important things go on in this class and there is no time to waste, your students will quickly settle down and be both respectful and ready to learn. Take attendance and pass out papers while they are reading or working at their desks; to allow them to sit idly by while you perform routine tasks will only encourage talking, joking and, ultimately, chaos. On the other hand, if they are working right away because you consistently start class immediately *every day*, you will avoid the biggest obstacle to good classroom management.

THE FIRST DAY OF SCHOOL

1. First, make sure the students know they are in the right place. Welcome them by introducing yourself very briefly. Briefly identify the class and stress the importance of this course, then get them seated in an order that makes sense to you.

I ask the students to sit in alphabetical order—just until I can recognize them in the halls (and that usually takes only a few days, even with 150+ students). I accomplish this by simply taking the attendance roster and calling out the names as I walk down the aisles, touching the desks to indicate where each student is to sit. Once they are all in their assigned seats (and I do this fast, so they don't have a chance to do anything but sit as quickly as I am moving), I then proceed to connect names and faces. I spend quite a bit of time learning to pronounce their names correctly, inventing some little mnemonic device to help me, and actually looking at each student individually. The investment of time pays off in huge dividends when I can call them by name almost immediately and they feel recognized and acknowledged.

2. **Next, ask the students to introduce themselves— on paper.** I pass out 3-by-5-inch index cards and ask each student to fill out one with his or her name, address, and a telephone number where the student can be reached in the evenings or where someone can take a message (in case the family has no telephone). They should also give the names of their parents/guardians and a daytime telephone number for them. I also ask them to write their birthdate in the upper right-hand corner. (I tell them I might want to bake them a cake, and I actually will make a big deal out of their birthday somehow—by singing to them probably.) At the bottom of the card they should let me know of any special needs they might have, such as physical problems (for example, allergies, epilepsy, nearsightedness, deafness, diabetes), learning difficulties and preferred learning styles, or anything they would like me to know about them that would help me teach them more effectively. (Sometimes, they will share the heartache of a recent death or divorce, maybe even "I'm pregnant," but usually comments are more in the vein of "I need lots of attention" or "I hate to read.")

3. While the students are passing their cards forward, **take some time to introduce yourself.** Students want to know a little bit about you and what to expect. Take some time to establish yourself in their eyes—your pro-

fessional preparation, background, and experience—even your family situation if you feel comfortable sharing a little personal information (not too much—just enough to establish some rapport as a person).

4. **Then, discuss the course content.** Describe how the year is going to shape up, what areas will be covered, what skills will be emphasized, and what they can expect to be doing in this class for the next nine months. The requirements for passing the class, the course syllabus, an assignment calendar, and any special materials they will need should be in writing and sent home with them.

5. **Remember to go over school regulations,** student handbooks, and required procedures. Discuss fire drill procedures, use of the hall pass, tardies, and other school rules you must enforce. Discuss the importance of following the same rules that everybody must obey in order to have a smoothly running building and a safe learning environment. Don't spend an undue amount of time on these regulations, but stress their importance to the total efficiency of the school.

6. **Finally, explain any specific rules or requests** you might have and why it is in their best interest to accommodate these public courtesies and universal expectations:

- keeping the room clean
- treating everyone with respect (no name calling, put-downs, or invading each other's space)
- giving their best effort

These are all expectations they can have of the teacher as well. I give them a little pep talk at this point about what they can look forward to with me as their teacher: I will always be prepared to teach them; I will never deliberately embarrass them or betray their confidence; I will do my best to live up to the trust they and their parents have placed in me. I talk about giving their best this year and that I will do everything in my power to help them pass this class: to understand the material, to improve their skills, and to broaden their horizons. I reassure them and I challenge them.

If you are not able to get through all of this on the first day, be sure to pay attention to the time, so that you can bring closure and end the class yourself rather than having them react to the bell. (Train them from the first day that you—not the bell—dismiss them.) Explain what you will be going over tomorrow, assure them you are looking forward to working with them, and then dismiss them within a few seconds after the bell.

You're off and running!

HOW TO COMMUNICATE WITH PARENTS AND THE WORLD AT LARGE

You are education's best public relations specialist. Let parents (and the world!) know what is going on in your classroom.

Contact parents frequently and in a variety of ways:
- Call immediately if there is a problem or concern. Handle problems quickly before they become real obstacles to learning.

- Send home frequent grade reports.
- Call soon after school begins simply to introduce yourself and to make contact.
- Send out postcards of praise.
- Utilize (or help establish) a twenty-four-hour computerized telephone hot line for grades and attendance.
- Schedule regular and frequent parent conferences.
- Send home notes, newsletters, and flyers.
- Take advantage of any televised programs that might be available through your school's or school district's media center to publicize events, activities, and accomplishments.
- Notify the local news media about upcoming special events or items of special interest.
- Send in items about your students for news stories; send letters to the editor from your students to local newspapers and radio and television stations.

Be sure your communication is error free and professionally presented:

- Proofread for grammar and spelling mistakes. Have someone else (a colleague or other "critical friend") read for clarity and overlooked errors.
- Be accurate with times, dates, location, and other facts.
- Make your written communication clear and legible. Type whenever possible.
- Keep it concise and to the point.

- When sending out permission slips, grade reports, and announcements, be sure to use a form that is easy to read.
- Avoid jargon.

Set up an accountability system:
- Keep a copy for your records (on a computer disc is best, but a hard-copy file or notebook is good, too).
- Give a copy to the office secretary, attendance clerk, and any other school personnel affected—and especially to your administrator.
- Keep a computer log of oral communications (telephone conversations, in-person conferences, discipline problems, funding requests for materials, incidents of harassment, vandalism, violence, suspicion of child abuse, neglect, or drug abuse).
- Set up a system for filing responses, replies, and permission slips. (Folders work well; they can be kept as long as necessary and then simply emptied when the contents, such as permission slips, are no longer pertinent.)

TIME-, ENERGY-, AND SANITY-SAVING TIPS

Paper Grading
Do it now! Check daily work immediately. Students need instant reinforcement and teachers need to stay caught up on their paperwork. Doing it now prevents having to take it home later.

Have students grade their own (or each other's) daily work whenever possible. Not only does this practice save the teacher hours of work, but students get immediate feedback and the review provides another teachable moment.

Require students to use a colored pen or pencil (different from that used to do the work) to mark papers.

Show students how to figure their own grades—regardless of the subject matter, they can always use the math practice! Ask them to write—clearly and legibly, at the top of the paper—the grade and the name of the person who did the checking .

Have students turn in workbooks opened to the correct pages so that you don't have to locate the work in order to grade and/or record the points.

Occasionally, you may even ask students to respond to a quick roll call with their scores, so that you can immediately record them. (If a student doesn't want to say the grade out loud, make it clear that any student may simply come show you the paper—perhaps to clarify a grade—in order to preserve confidentiality when that is important.)

If students check each other's work, require them to hand papers back to their owners for review and verification. They will most often stringently challenge any discrepancy and question any ambiguous wording, and—once again—increase and deepen their understanding of the material even more.

Always have students pass in the corrected papers for you to review. Then, do a quick, random visual check for accuracy and honesty. Not every paper needs to be rechecked every time, and students won't know whether their individual paper is being reviewed. A periodic check, an occasional teacher correction, or written comment will let students know that you are checking papers and will minimize carelessness and outright cheating.

Use sticky notes for corrections and comments attached to student papers to minimize teacher marks on student work and to encourage their revisions.

Utilize lay graders: Whenever possible, take advantage of outside graders if they are available in your area. Lay graders are trained readers who usually have a degree in English or a related field or who are themselves good writers with excellent proofreading skills. By sending them essays to be graded before you read them, you save yourself hours of time-consuming detail reading. The lay grader can check for mechanics, organization, and sentence construction and development, allowing you to focus your own reading on the content and the specifics of the assignment.

Whether or not you are a language arts teacher, there will undoubtedly be times when you will make writing assignments and probably would do so more often if you could get them graded in a timely fashion. By incorporating lay graders (who are usually hired, trained, and paid for through district language arts curriculum specialists) into your plan, you can make more writing assignments and still keep up with the grading.

Teacher Grading Systems

Some work must be graded by the teacher alone because of its complexity or confidentiality. In that case, whether you stay at school to do your grading or take it home, do it in a timely fashion— preferably the day it was turned in.

Work out a system that works for you. Many teachers prefer to take a break and come back to the paper-grading later in the day or evening. Many prefer to stay at their desks, get it done and leave it at school. Whatever your preference—and it may change as your responsibilities change, whether they be family obligations, extracurricular duties, or personal commitments—stay on top of it. Doing your paperwork immediately keeps you up-to-date, always aware of your students' progress, and organized. Your students will know that their work is important and will get timely feedback.

Alternate classes or groups for lengthy projects or those that involve bulky materials. Sometimes it is easier planning to keep everybody together, doing the same assignments at the same time, but weigh the benefits of being able to get a smaller number of big projects evaluated and returned to the students quickly, and being able to display them adequately, with the convenience of having all your students doing every assignment at the same time.

Not every assignment needs to be turned in. Check over student work in progress. Papers done during guided practice may not need to be graded, but may simply be checked and sent home or placed in the student's notebook or portfolio immediately.

Use a scanner for scoring tests whenever possible. It will save hours of grading time. Most media centers or copier labs in individual schools have one available for your use. If not, check with your district's central administration office, district media center, or teacher resource center.

Use the computer, if you have one available in your classroom, for recording evaluations of oral presentations. Your comments can be entered immediately during your observation of the student's presentation, just like they would be if they were handwritten; the main differences are that not only will the printed form be legible, but you will be able to make more comments (if you type faster than you write), you won't have to look away from the student's presentation so often (if you can touch-type), you will have a permanent record of your evaluation, and the student will have immediate feedback. (One major caveat, however: Always, always, always make a backup disc of everything you do on the computer!)

Buy rubber stamps with often-repeated comments such as "Sign and Return," "Redo," "Save," or any other instructions that meet your personal requirements for student work.

Recording grades can be done in a variety of ways; some general guidelines apply to all disciplines, however. Using a grade book with handwritten records will probably always be a good backup; however, using the computer is the most time-efficient and accurate way to keep track of students' grades. If grades are entered under categories that correspond to the standards students are supposed to meet, requirements for both class credit and standard completion will be recorded in the same place. Students will be able to see immediately the connection between assignments and content standards. The teacher can always give the students and/or their parents up-to-date progress reports, and at the end of the grading period, the final grade is already figured! Just be sure you always make a backup disc. To enter all this data for over 150 students, only to lose it in an electrical blink of the computer's eye, would be devastating.

Following is a grade printout for one student's work during one semester. It shows the standard to be met as the category. The assignments are listed underneath, along with the possible points and the points the student earned, which are then computed to a percentage and a letter grade. Whether a student meets the district standard (in our case, a score of 5 for some, and a 75% for others) can be determined by referring to the actual score received on the assessment or to the category average (if it is 75% or better the student has succeeded).

FIGURE 3-4
GRADE PRINTOUT

Student Summary for Freshman English/Spring 1996
FINAL GRADE REPORT FOR ENGLISH 9
SPRING SEMESTER, 1995-1996
LINCOLN JR. HIGH/PAT WOODWARD, TEACHER

Student Name	Final Grade	Total Points
JOE STUDENT	B (91.806)	3328/3625

Notes: JOE HAS SUCCESSFULLY MET ALL FRESHMAN ENGLISH STANDARDS

CLEAR WRITING (950) category average: 86%

Punctuation Review	(50)	50	100%	A
Punctuation Quiz	(50)	50	100%	A
Capitalization Review	(50)	50	100%	A
Capitalization Quiz	(50)	50	100%	A
Daily Oral Language	(100)	70	70%	C
Editorial Analysis	(50)	45	90%	A
Editorial	(100)	78	78%	C
Essay (informative)	(100)	94	94%	A
Essay (explanation)	(100)	88	88%	B
Essay (opinion)	(100)	90	90%	A
Essay (process)	(100)	92	92%	A
Essay (argument)	(100)	90	90%	A
Expository Essay Standard	(5)	7	140%	A
Persuasive Essay Standard	(5)	6	120%	A
Literary Analysis Essay	(100)	93	93%	A
Formal Letter	(100)	100	100%	A

LITERARY TERMS AND TECHNIQUES (950) category average: 88.7%

"Romeo and Juliet" vocabulary	(50)	48	96%	A
Drama terms test	(100)	92	92%	A
Poetry terms test	(100)	97	97%	A
Free verse	(100)	95	95%	A
Ballad	(100)	96	96%	A
Heritage poem (original)	(100)	90	90%	A
Choice poem (original)	(100)	50	50%	F
Sonnet analysis	(100)	86	86%	B
Original sonnet	(100)	88	88%	B
Poetry terms test	(100)	97	97%	A

CONTRIBUTIONS OF KEY WRITERS (626 category average: 89.4%

Maya Angelou Report (researched)	(100)	91	91%	A
Truman Capote Report (researched)	(100)	93	93%	A
Robert Frost Report (researched)	(100)	90	90%	A
Shakespeare Report (researched)	(100)	88	88%	B
e. e. cummings Report (researched)	(100)	78	78%	C
Author of choice report (researched)	(100)	86	86%	B
Brought in or sang ballads	(100)	100	100%	A

RESEARCH (543) category average: 90.3%

Preliminary bibliography	(25)	20	80%	B
Preliminary outline	(25)	23	92%	A
Notecards	(50)	45	90%	A
Final outline	(50)	50	100%	A
Rough draft	(100)	90	90%	A
Final bibliography	(50)	45	90%	A
Documented essay	(300)	270	90%	A

CREATIVE WRITING (280) category average: 95%

Daily journal entries	(100)	100	100%	A
Poetry notebook	(200)	180	90%	A

FORMAL LETTER (150) category average: 10%

Letter of request	(50)	50	100%	A
Letter of application	(50)	50	100%	A
Letter of recommendation	(50)	50	100%	A

EXTRA CREDIT (50)

Assignment calendar posted	(10)	10	100%	A
Mid-hexter returned	(10)	10	100%	A
Shakespeare wordsearch	(10)	10	100%	A
Extra shakespeare project	(10)	20	200%	A
Speech contest	(10)	?	?	
Essay contest	(10)	?	?	
Short story contest	(10)	?	?	
Brought in ballads	(10)	?	?	
Brought in music	(10)	?	?	
Performed ballad	(10)	?	?	

Student responsibility for saving work: After reviewing, grading, and/or recording student corrected work, return it to the student. Never throw away work that has been counted for a grade. Make the student responsible for saving it to prevent confusion over whether a grade is correct, especially at the secondary level where the stakes for meeting graduation requirements are especially high. A good policy for both the teacher and the students is that a score must be recorded, and/or the student must have the hard copy (the original work) for the grade to count. Explain to students that teachers do—occasionally—make mistakes: a grade can be left out or recorded for the wrong student; if this happens, you will cheerfully correct the mistake, *if the student can provide the original graded paper.* If he or she doesn't have it, and the teacher has no record of the grade, what's a body to do? You can't invent a grade. Teach your students to hang on to graded work, because it functions just like a receipt—and we should always save receipts!

A place for everything: Put all student work of the same kind in one place—the same safe, convenient place.

Keep student paperwork for each class in its own folder. Put all class members' written work in this folder immediately. As soon as it is reviewed and recorded, put it back into the folder, only to be taken out when it is returned to the students.

Keep students' bulky notebooks or journals in plastic baskets, sturdy cardboard boxes, or file cabinets. Take them out only to check or return them.

Keep portfolios in the classroom. Wall baskets or portable filing baskets (plastic or heavy cardboard), marked by period and by alphabet (A - L, M - Z), aid in keeping portfolios or other important student documents protected and organized.

Have a place for big projects to be displayed—shelves designed for this purpose, display cases, bulletin boards, or wall space set aside for posters, paintings, and other large visuals will show off student work. You can even have students be responsible for choosing and displaying their own outstanding work and, thus, create a student-generated bulletin board or room decor that they will take pride in while saving you work.

Little tricks of the trade:

- Use magnets to stick papers to chalkboards—they're cleaner and faster than tape.
- Make extra copies of everything in case you need them for new students, to replace lost papers, or for reteaching. Keep them in specially marked folders.
- Copy handouts on a different color for each subject or class, or quickly mark the edge of each stack with a different colored marker for easy identification.
- Provide scratch pads made from recycled paper for students to use in thinking, pop quizzes, and sponge activities (those quick learning activities prepared and ready to productively use those extra minutes which occasionally happen during the day or at the end of a period).
- Mark a master copy with a sticker or colored mark in the top corner to prevent your using it as a handout or giving it away.

- Write your daily plan for the next day on the board before you leave each day; not only will you feel more prepared when you walk in the door, you will be ready for any emergency or delay that can cost you valuable early-morning moments.

- If you know you are going to be absent the next day, write out plans for a substitute as you go through the day. Key information will be fresh on your mind, and the task of writing out your plans won't be so time-consuming if broken into little chunks throughout the day.

- Write it down! Write down appointments, meetings, conferences—everything—on the same calendar.

- Get in the habit of keeping notes. Write notes to yourself when you need to remember something out of the ordinary; have students write you a note when they want you to do them a favor; make lists of chores to do and mark them off as you complete them; jot down good ideas as they occur to you; keep records of student discipline incidents on the computer; write out that good idea that worked so well in class today—you will want to repeat it!

- Pay attention to what other teachers do and ask to share their ideas. Don't be afraid to share your own. Take time to talk to each other!

A SMORGASBORD OF SUGGESTIONS
FOR PASSING OUT PAPERS

Pass back papers while students are doing quiet seat work. At the beginning of the term, this also helps you learn their names more quickly.

Have a student pass out papers to be returned during seat time (when the class is getting ready for an activity, reading required material, or doing quiet work in preparation for the lesson).

Teach students to pick up their own papers and supplies. Have a place where students may routinely pick up graded work or supplied materials or handouts for the day. Clearly marked trays, baskets, and other areas that indicate needed supplies or printed work will facilitate student independence and a quick class start. This will take some consistent practice at first, but when students see that you expect them to take care of their own needs, you will save valuable time otherwise spent in handing out things.

Pass out handouts (when you must) by counting the number of students in a row or area as you are counting the papers to be distributed; hand the stack to the student nearest you and ask him or her to pass them back. As a habit, don't take the time to walk around and individually give students materials, worksheets, or tests. It is time-consuming and inefficient, unless you are checking on other work at the same time or giving specific, individual instructions or comments.

Have row captains or group leaders routinely pick up any papers and other materials for the other students.

Arrange handouts for easy access and expect students to be sure everyone is prepared before the activity begins.

Write the names of absent students on handouts. Either keep them in a special folder or have another student keep them and explain the assignment to the absent student when he/she returns.

Plastic baskets not only provide excellent storage for bulky folders and workbooks, but they are also useful for handing out science or art materials.

Honor the "no talking" rule while papers are being collected or handed back to avoid having to restore order later. Use this time to talk to the class yourself, make comments on the general quality of their work, or ask questions.

MISCELLANEOUS MINUTE-SAVERS THAT CAN SAVE YOU HOURS

Return all telephone calls after school. Only emergency calls should interrupt class time.

Put all newsletters, permission slips, announcements, tests, assignments, calendars, and worksheets on the computer. You can make corrections each time you use them, and you won't need to re-create them from scratch every year.

Write the day's date and assignment in the same place on the board every morning before school starts (or every afternoon before you leave for the day, so it's ready when you—or a substitute, should you need one—gets there).

Use a stamp with your signature for cumulative

folders, portfolios, and daily progress reports, to cut down on hundreds of repetitive signings.

Use hand signals rather than voice commands whenever possible. Students will learn to watch for them and you will not have to raise your voice to get their attention.

On the first day of school, have each student fill out a student information card (see page 52). Take these cards home and use them to make notes whenever you call a student's home or need quick information about a student.

Collect and use sponge activities whenever those extra five minutes of otherwise free time occur. You can reinforce student learning through a group game, a quick puzzle, or a mind-bending riddle. By taking advantage of those extra five minutes a day, you can gain two to three *days* of instruction time during a school year.

Whenever a student asks you to repeat instructions, call on another student to do so. Ask a student to repeat directions before beginning to double-check for understanding and clarification.

Do as much work at school as possible. You'll have easier access to records and student files and will feel less stressed if you don't have to do it at home.

Team teach whenever possible. Plan with other teachers and teach your strength by rotating responsibilities. Ensure that all the students get the same information the same way.

If you team teach, hold parent conferences with your teaching partner; this practice will save time and double the impact.

Divide duties between team teachers: Whenever possible, rotate writing newsletter articles, announcements to send home, planning units, ordering films, materials, supplies, and supervising activities.

Grade a few papers every day rather than saving it for the weekend (when you have other things to do!).

Color-code your grade book according to subject, class, units, hexters, quarters, even assignments to make information retrieval possible at a glance.

Space the collection of big assignments over several days so that you don't have all projects turned in at the same time. Avoid collecting lots of work on Friday.

Use volunteers to help call parents for work on various projects.

Have a personal bulletin board above your desk for important notices, lists, family photos, student notes, even a flyswatter!

Create working bulletin boards by having the students display their work.

Paper clip or band all papers from one assignment together, so that you don't have to sort later in order to grade and record.

Keep your committee work to a minimum. Learn to say "no" unless you really are committed to a cause and want to work for it.

Check over your mail as soon as you pick it up, throwing out what doesn't interest you or demand your attention. Make note of important dates and discard any mail you don't have to save. Do not let it pile up.

Start on time! Teachers who habitually take five or ten minutes to get started lose two to five days a year just by not being ready to begin class when the bell rings.

Prioritize. Decide what is important and spend your energy on the essentials. Pick your battles.

Let the little stuff slide. If an activity or demand has little or no educational value and you don't have to do it, learn to say "no."

DISCIPLINE DO's AND DON'T's

Do:

Be someone students can trust: Keep their secrets if at all possible and maintain their confidence in your ability to be in charge. Students need to feel safe and have reasonable boundaries.

Be their friend, but not their buddy: Many beginning teachers confuse being a friend with being a peer. They try to act like their students, win their approval by being one of them, even socialize with them. The end result will almost always be a loss, if not completely disastrous, for both teacher and students. Being a friend means being supportive, friendly, trustworthy. For the teacher, it does not mean being one of the gang. Work on maintaining a professional distance while at the same time being an adult your students trust and like to be around.

Be willing to laugh with your students: If you can't enjoy your students and their personalities, you are in the wrong field! There is nothing wrong with having fun with your students, and being able to see the humor in a situation can be incredibly valuable. Many a tense moment or potential blowup has been lightened by a quick joke or a little genuine humor—not laughing at a student, but being able to laugh with them at a situation. If they are being funny, acknowledge it, and enjoy it!

Be clear and simple in stating your expectations: Don't make them guess. Say what you mean clearly and succinctly and match your voice and facial expression to your statements. Students shouldn't have to figure out your mood in order to know what to expect.

Be consistent: Train your students. Inconsistent responses to their behavior, especially at the beginning of the year, will cause them to be confused and will, in fact, encourage the very behavior you don't want.

Be firm but fair: Don't bend the rules for some but not for others. This is not to say that everyone must be treated the same, but the same standards for behavior should apply to everyone. For example, until someone abuses the privilege, everyone should be allowed to use the hall pass, but only those who can handle the responsibility (by not asking too frequently, by coming back promptly, and so on) should continue to be given the privilege.

Encourage your students to help establish the norms for classroom behavior: When students are involved in setting expectations for themselves, when they have input to offer the behavior agreement, there will be better participation than when the teacher lays down the rules. Plus, students will usually be stricter and harder on themselves than you would be!

Agree on a few simple rules: It's tempting for students to try to come up with a rule for every little thing, and pretty soon you're down to "Please don't eat the daisies." If you can get them to agree on the most basic rules, however, it's much easier to enforce a few important laws than it is to keep track of many little regulations.

Keep an orderly classroom: A well-organized, neat classroom encourages responsible behavior. When they come into the room, if the desks are in disarray and the floor is cluttered, their attitude will quickly reflect their surroundings. Involve students in keeping the room clean, and require them to clean up after themselves as a matter of habit.

Know your students: First, learn their names. Spend as much time as necessary learning to match names with faces. Come up with a quick mnemonic device to help you remember names and correct pronunciations. Call the students by their preferred names (if appropriate!) and be sure you don't mispronounce them. One way to learn their names within two or three days, especially in the upper grades, is to have them sit in alphabetical order—just until you can really call them by their names. (See p.51.) Make a big deal out of knowing who they are and wanting to recognize them as individuals.

Then, as you get to know them better, pay attention to their needs and to their moods, and you can often anticipate situations and prevent trouble. Greet them at the door when they arrive, make sure you make eye contact with every student. Try to give individual attention to some degree to every student every day.

Involve your students: When students are busy learning and participating, they are less likely to find distractions and indulge in inappropriate activity. The more interesting and varied the activities, the more the students will become engaged in productive activity.

Include everyone: Be aware of students with special needs and be prepared to accommodate them.

Let your students know you care about them: Praise in public and punish in private. A sincere compliment, a quick comment made quietly one-on-one, a concerned inquiry, a gentle reminder, a pat on the shoulder can often accomplish much more than a lecture or a sermon.

Focus on the behavior, not the person: Reinforce the behavior you want to encourage and ignore the behavior you want to eliminate (unless it is dangerous or openly defiant and disrespectful).

Don't:

Threaten: Warnings should be kept simple and as private as possible. A whisper, a look, a hand signal, are all valuable discipline tools.

Lecture: Talking too much diminishes impact. Use signals whenever possible; making a circling motion with your hand works as well as or better than saying "Turn around."

Humiliate: Never, by name-calling or even by a look, cause a student to lose self-esteem.

Argue: A discussion in private may work wonders, but an argument, particularly in front of others, will only escalate a discipline problem.

Embarrass: Matching wits with a student, pointing out a student's shortcomings, or alluding to a student's personal life, will only escalate (or, worse, create) a discipline problem.

Yell: A low voice and a firm tone, matched with a serious expression, will be much more effective than raising your voice and losing your cool.

Touch a student in anger: Not only will this be grounds for a lawsuit in many states, but it is dangerous for both the teacher and the student.

Open-Door Policy

A word of caution: Many teachers have become, and justifiably so, wary about touching students at all. Depending upon the age of the student, the teaching style of the adult, and the situation, hugs and touches need not be forbidden. Touching anyone you do not know well is probably not a good idea, but there are times when a hand on the shoulder, a friendly shoulder hug, or a pat on the back is exactly what is called for.

Nevertheless, we can all take some simple steps to protect not only our students but our own reputations by developing an "open-door" policy:

- Teach with your door open whenever possible.
- Always leave the door open when working with individual students.
- Encourage drop-in visits from other teachers and administrators.
- Ask parents (and grandparents!) to observe, tutor, and chaperone students in your classroom.
- Avoid giving rides to students or being alone with them away from the school.

- Avoid singling out certain students for special treats or privileges (in other words, be careful not to "play favorites").
- Keep your comments friendly, supportive, encouraging, and appropriate. Ask yourself whether this conversation, behavior, or response is one that this child's parents would approve of.

GETTING READY FOR A SUB

Having students absent is tough enough, but when the teacher is gone, things really get complicated. Most teachers will go to school even when they shouldn't; when they are sick enough to be in bed, they will crawl their way to their students, believing that they really need to be there. They don't want to lose a moment, let alone a day or two, of valuable instructional time, and believe (with some justification!) that their presence is necessary to the students' learning. They don't want any interruption of the flow, they don't want students to be confused or lose momentum, they just don't want to miss out on anything! Nevertheless, teachers do become ill occasionally, or are faced with a family emergency, and once in a while they may need to attend a professional conference.

When an absence is necessary, a teacher must call for a substitute. Be sure to follow your school's established protocol for getting a sub. Don't take it upon yourself to call your own sub unless this has been approved by your school district. Most schools, at least larger ones, have a procedure that involves a designated school official and a district substitute coordinator. Depending on whether the absence is a planned one or an unforeseen emergency, you need to give as much advance notification as possible. If it is a planned absence, be sure to fill out the necessary paperwork as far ahead as you can to be sure your request is filled to your satisfaction.

If you can request a specific substitute, and you have found one you trust and feel comfortable with, all the better. Whether you know the person who is filling in for you or not, be sure to leave complete, detailed plans. Once these are on your computer, they can be easily updated whenever you must be away. Highlight or boldface key words, phrases, and times.

Remember to include:

- The daily schedule complete with specific times and divisions of activities or classes. Be sure to include the students' routine, where each activity takes place and how long it should take.
- Up-to-date and accurate seating charts. It helps to include a phonetic spelling to aid in pronunciation of unusual student names.
- Attendance sheets with necessary specific instructions on taking roll and any legal documentation, such as signing on that day's attendance. Be sure to tell the sub not only when and how to take attendance, but what to do with the forms once they are completed.
- A brief explanation of previous instruction

and/or activities and how the day's lessons and work fit into the unit. This gives the sub some sense of continuity and perspective and will help him bring his own expertise to the class. He will be able to answer questions better if he knows how today's assignment fits into the overall scheme.

- Specific instructions for class activities and student expectations. Be sure to include clear, step-by-step sequences. Don't leave out anything! Knowing how the VCR works or being able to open a certain cabinet or closet will probably be crucial to the success of the lesson, so double-check that you have left everything in order, down to the smallest detail.

- Location of books, folders, papers, administrative forms such as office referrals, passes to the nurse, media center, restroom, locker, and so on. Clearly mark samples of the textbooks students will be using and administrative folders containing forms or student work with stick-on notes, and put them in an impossible-to-miss spot on your desk. Don't forget to point out where the students' materials and books are located.

- Brief instructions on how to help students catch up who have been absent, should they return during your absence.

- Clear instructions for using passes, according privileges, and classroom behavior. Be sure to specify what is and is not allowed. If you don't permit gum or food in the classroom, say so. Don't set up the sub by omitting this little piece of information, because, invariably, some student will say, "But Mrs. Conrad lets us do it."

Prepare your students for your absence well in advance, even when you don't know when you might be gone. In other words, don't wait until you have to be out to get your students ready for the inevitable absence. Let them know what your expectations of them are for how to treat guests in the classroom. A substitute is best received when viewed as a guest teacher, and when students are briefed as to what behavior is expected of them. If possible, invite guests into your classroom for sessions with your students while you are also there. Review with them your expectations and encourage them to come up with creative ways to make new people feel comfortable. Rewards for positive feedback usually result in continued good behavior!

The School

WHO'S WHO?
PEOPLE AND PLACES TO KNOW

School buildings are often so big nowadays that the faculty and staff are probably no longer small and personally acquainted. It's easy to come into a school as a new teacher and not get to know the person who teaches at the other end of the building for another five years. Sometimes we wonder who on earth all these people are whose names are on mailboxes, and more puzzling yet is what on earth they do. Then, there's the central office (or "downtown," as some teachers call that building where central administration is housed), and that can remain a mystery for an entire career if you're not particularly interested. Some educators go into their classrooms as beginning teachers and never come out until they retire. They don't know who the other teachers are, don't care about the services provided at the district level, and aren't interested in the support available at the state and national levels. Thankfully, they are not typical of our profession. To prevent becoming one of these blinder-wearing recluses, take the time to figure out who you should know and where to go to get the help you need. Each building has its own needs and consequently has its own staff and faculty makeup; you might find a dean of students in one building and a registrar in another, while one school may employ a community relations officer and another will need a student services coordinator. The following list includes the most commonly found employees in many school districts.

Start with Your Own Building

The Principal: The head of an elementary or secondary school, this person is the educational leader of a team of education specialists, and is responsible for the curriculum, extracurricular activities, support systems, budget and personnel decisions, communications with parents and district school administration officials, and day-to-day operations of the school. The principal has administrative certification and is responsible for the overall supervision of every aspect of delivering the total educational program. The principal is your education team member, your mentor, and your advocate, as well as your supervisor. Establish and maintain close communications and a friendly relationship with this person.

Assistant principal: As the "second in command," this job title might be shared by several people who are responsible for various aspects of running a large school. Comparable to a vice president in the corporate world, this individual or team shares the administrative responsibilities of the principal and they cooperate to perform the many duties of the office. The advice for working relationships and rapport with the assistant principal are the same as those for the principal.

Dean of students: A member of the administrative leadership team, also with administrative credentials, the dean of students is typically responsible for student activities, and in many schools is designated as the activities director. Extracurricular activities, discipline, facilitating and implementing student programs, counseling students and student groups, and maintaining good student body communications are usually the primary responsibilities of the dean (often an assistant principal assumes these roles if there is no dean of students). The dean (or assistant principal) can run interference for you, help you hurdle obstacles, give you information, and help establish smooth operations.

Counselor: In many schools the counselors are also members of the administrative leadership team. They have special certification and training to counsel students academically and personally. They facilitate class schedules, advise students academically, and provide emotional and psychological support. Many times you will act as a counselor to your students because that's part of the nature of the job, but remember that the professional in the counselor's office is there for a reason.

Do not try to solve all the problems of the world your-self. Make referrals when the occasion calls for them and enlist the professional expertise of the one trained to provide this service. Know when you *must* call on the counselor: in situations of abuse, neglect, or emotional or physical trauma. Know the legal ramifications of these situations and talk to the counselor frequently. This person will help you know your students and pro-vide the services they need. Together, you will be the team your students need.

School psychologist: Specially trained to work with young people and their families, school psychologists evaluate and determine the needs and programs for stu-dents who are experiencing more severe emotional and psychological problems. They often work with coun-selors and social workers in several different schools.

Social worker: Social work professionals work with students with special needs and with their families, often in conjunction with outside agencies such as Child Protective Services, Family Assistance, Child Support Enforcement Administration, and other state social ser-vices agencies or departments.

School nurse: Sometimes an aide or a paraprofes-sional, this is most often a trained nurse with both nurs-ing and teaching degrees, who may serve several schools. The nurse is responsible for treating and refer-ring medical emergencies, health-related testing, and maintenance of student health records.

Speech pathologist/therapist: This specially trained and certified staff member works with students who have speech impairments or difficulties. This professional is qualified to diagnose and provide treatment for a number of speech and hearing problems and will provide testing for all students and training for staff as well as individual therapy. Several schools often share the services of one therapist.

Occupational therapist: This specially trained and certified staff member most often works with students who have physical disabilities. The occupational therapist is qualified to diagnose and provide treatment for a number of problems and will also often provide training for staff as well as individual therapy and specialized equipment for students who need their services. Again, several schools usually share the services of one therapist.

Librarian/media specialist: The media specialist is a certified teacher who specializes in library science and technology-assisted media. This faculty member will order, maintain, and provide materials and equipment for students and teachers. He or she will provide instruction whenever appropriate and provide curriculum and technology assistance in every discipline. The librarian/media specialist is a teacher's and a student's best friend!

Secretary/office manager: One of the most powerful and influential individuals in the school, this person holds the key not only to the supply closet, but quite possibly to your future. She or he is privy to practically everything that goes on in the building and most likely the district, and is responsible for the smooth running of the school. Everything from arranging for substitutes, buses, office equipment and supplies, supervision of all record keeping, paying bills and handing out paychecks, plus myriad responsibilities the principal assigns fall on this overworked and too often underappreciated super-human. Be solicitous, be nice, be cooperative, be responsible—do whatever it takes to be sure you help the office manager, because he or she can certainly help you. Anything you want or need in the way of providing a service to your students will probably go across this desk, and the impression you make on the person who runs it will undoubtedly be conveyed to the principal in one way or another—to say nothing of how helpful the office manager can be to you on a daily basis.

Custodian: Another person who has an impact on how well you can do your job and how pleasant your surroundings (working conditions) are is the custodian. Custodians don't just sweep the floor and empty the trash: they maintain all physical aspects of the building and have influence over the types of activities that take place in your room. Remember that they have an important job to do and we shouldn't make it harder by increasing their workload. Without their services, your program and, ultimately, your students suffer.

Cook: Obviously, this person provides one of the school's most important support services in the eyes of the students, and quite possibly the cook has much greater clout than you might at first realize. The time lunch is to be served might well determine the schedule for the whole school. Whether or not an activity conflicts with lunchtime can impact its success or failure. If you plan a field trip that will take students away at lunchtime, be sure you include the lunchroom staff in your planning. Let the cooks know when your activities will have a bearing on their lunch count. These administrative details are important.

Paraprofessional: The aides at every level and in every capacity make many programs possible in these overburdened times. Paraprofessionals may not have the same training as teachers, but they do have training and experience and a willingness to help that makes them indispensable to teachers. Unlike volunteers, they get paid for their services and most teachers come to depend on them as their right arms. They are most often employed in special education classes, special programs, and large classes. Be sure to work closely with paraprofessionals and provide as much training and support as possible for them, and you will double the educational impact of every program or classroom where they are employed.

Volunteer: Most often parents, but occasionally other community members or grandparents, volunteers make teachers' jobs possible—or at least, they certainly ease the workload. They will work with groups, tutor individuals, perform clerical duties—just about anything you ask of them. Remember to let them know exactly how they can best help you help the students and they will bend over backward to accomplish it. Most volunteers appreciate having specific tasks and scheduled times to work. Knowing how to work with volunteers is an art that requires planning time and careful organization with the individual volunteer, but the time invested in preparation pays off huge dividends in student achievement and self-confidence. Be creative in thinking of ways volunteers can help, and engage individual volunteers in brainstorming ideas. Then, really use them—they want to be useful!

District Offices

Next, familiarize yourself with the central administration office or student support services center for your district. Who works there and what do they do? The positions required by school districts may vary from area to area, and often the duties of one title might be assumed or shared by another. Frequently, the responsibilities outlined in a job description in one area are often attributed to another title in some other district (or even in another building in the same district). For example, a principal in Colorado might be called a headmaster in another state, particularly in a private school system, and the same tendency is true at the central administration level. Consequently, the following descriptions are broad, with the intention of conveying a sense of what these jobs entail, rather than providing a detailed description of their specific responsibilities.

Superintendent: The chief administrator of a school system, the superintendent is responsible for implementing the school board's policies, rules and regulations, and enforcing state and federal mandates, as well as representing the school district as its educational leader and maintaining school, community, and board relations. There is a superintendent, sometimes called a commissioner, at the state level as well as in each local school district; the responsibilities are comparable, but at a statewide level are much broader in scope. This person is not inaccessible to you, and even though she or he, like the CEO of a major business, may seem far removed, the superintendent does, in fact as well as in theory, welcome your input more often than not. Do not be afraid to approach your superintendent (with an appointment, of course), if you have an idea or a concern you need to discuss at that level.

Assistant superintendent: One or several individuals may fill this administrative position, which serves to help fulfill the responsibilities of the superintendent, especially in larger school districts. This person may be responsible for any of the specific roles of the office of the superintendent and is often in charge of supervising one or more aspects of school district management, including finance, curriculum and program development, staffing and personnel development, and pupil personnel services. The assistant superintendent usually has close knowledge of the immediate concerns of individual schools and will often be a valuable resource to teachers as well as to building principals. Again, meet and confer when you need to.

Curriculum specialists: Educators with special training in curriculum development, these individuals work from the central administration offices with classroom teachers in planning, organizing, and developing curriculum in the content areas. They are a valuable resource to teachers, providing assistance in procuring materials, assisting in program articulation, and providing staff development. They are a teacher's greatest source of assistance with questions concerning materials, programs, or practices involving curriculum. Take advantage of their expertise in helping you plan and deliver your curriculum.

Personnel director: Often called a human resource officer, this is the individual in charge of providing a clearinghouse for applicants for and current employees in the various positions required by a school district. This office provides record maintenance and assistance in any of the many areas that affect the district's employees, including certification, licensure, insurance, and legal matters. The first person a potential candidate for employment meets, this individual (or individuals in the personnel office) remains crucial to the professional employment of every employee in the system. They can answer questions and provide assistance in a wide range of employee concerns and they are often the place to start in resolving questions surrounding employment issues.

Information systems director: As school districts become more technology-dependent, data collection and information retrieval become rapidly more sophisticated, requiring the guidance and expertise of individuals specially trained in computer technology. The director works specifically with the central office in designing, managing, and supervising programs and systems that provide technological support required by the overall operations of the school district. For teachers, this person may be quite removed from our day-to-day activities, but the information systems director does indeed provide assistance and support in the intricate workings of the technology that makes our jobs more efficient, businesslike, and ultimately, professionally effective.

Organizational or staff development director: This individual is responsible for planning, organizing, and implementing in-service programs, classes, training opportunities, seminars, and conferences that provide further education for district employees and may be required by the district. This office works with the total organization or system to provide districtwide staff development and cooperates with curriculum specialists and other district administrators to develop and deliver programs for its employees to promote district goals.

Media and technology support services director: Responsible for the acquisition, distribution, and maintenance of technology in the individual schools throughout the district, this office functions as a resource for the media specialists, teachers, and administrators, providing advice and services necessary for the efficient use of computers and other media technology. This person or this office will be the one who will assist building media specialists and technology specialists, who in turn assist and support teachers and administrators. They are the ones who keep us (our computers, anyway) up and running!

Accountability and assessment director: This individual oversees the testing and assessment of students throughout the district and reports required standardized test scores to the appropriate agencies and departments. This office is responsible for the supervision of state-mandated testing and ensuring that schools comply with state requirements and district objectives. Developing assessment tools in cooperation with curriculum specialists and classroom teachers and reporting student performance achievement and other pertinent statistics are this office's primary responsibilities.

Research and development director: This office develops programs, provides assistance in education research, and supervises innovative and pilot programs, as well as helps procure grants, research funds, and technological and human resources support for district administrators and individual schools. This office will provide resources for a wide variety of research in any academic or school-related area. Utilize their expertise whenever you need information regarding latest developments, research, or assistance in curriculum innovation.

Parent Groups

Be familiar with the parent groups in your district, such as the following.

Parent Teacher Association: The PTA is usually a fund-raising, spirit-boosting, school-supporting body of parents and teachers who come together to work for their individual schools. A national organization, with state and local affiliations, they have specific goals and requirements, carry substantial political clout, and are a powerful supporter of education. Dues, membership, activities, and responsibilities are governed at a national level with individual schools following their guidelines and requirements. They sponsor all kinds of student events, help chaperone activities, and provide classroom assistance in a variety of ways. They are invaluable!

Parent Teacher Organization: The PTO is similar to the PTA and originated as a less formal and less structured organization, usually with more autonomy and flexibility. Their purposes, goals, and objectives are similar to those of the PTA, with their main function being to support individual schools. Whether the parent/teacher group in your area is the PTA or a PTO, this partnership helps bring success to students.

Parent advisory boards: In some districts, parents serve in an advisory capacity to the administration and teachers of individual schools, functioning as a vital component of site-based management and shared decision making. They may be incorporated in a school improvement team or function as a separate entity. In either format, as parents they are shareholders in the business of education, and their input on curriculum, budget, and daily operations is not only valuable, but crucial to the success of their own children and of their school. They serve as volunteers and are committed to the excellence of education and the welfare of students. Go to their meetings whenever possible and engage them as partners in achieving your school's mission.

Local and State Boards

The local board of education: This important group has the final word in curriculum, staffing, budget, and educational policies. Members are sometimes appointed, but at the local level are normally elected. A chief school officer (often called a superintendent) is selected to implement their decisions. They are the most powerful elected body in the world of education and have an incredible influence on the educational outcome of a district's policies and programs as well as on the morale and environment of the whole system. After being elected by voters, usually to a four-year term, school board members volunteer their time and want to see their district succeed; they are usually quite open to teacher involvement and input. Bend their ears and keep them informed; that is the only way they will really be able to make informed decisions and provide the leadership a school district requires.

The State Board of Education: This group offers many services. It is made up of elected officials who perform the administrative tasks needed to implement state policy. They certify teachers, test student progress, provide information and training to teachers, distribute state and federal funds, oversee school districts' compliance with state laws, and conduct educational research and development. State departments staff offices and agencies that provide direct educational and staff development opportunities for recertification and for salary increases. It is your responsibility as a professional to take advantage of their services.

Professional associations: Finally, be aware of the many resources available to you through your teachers' association at the local, state, and national levels. A list of individual names here would be almost immediately obsolete, but keep abreast of who holds the various offices of agencies and associations that directly affect you. You can do this by reading professional journals and association publications, by attending conferences, and by staying professionally and politically involved. Know who the president of your local association is and call him or her with your concerns; write to your state representatives with your suggestions and ideas; vote for the officers of your professional organizations and associations because you know who they are and what they stand for, not just because you may recognize their names; provide the necessary touch with reality that these folks frequently require. Pay attention to what the U.S. Secretary of Education is doing.

For specific names and information on how to contact them, consult the *Directory of State Education Agencies,* listed in Appendix B.

The National Board for Professional Teaching Standards (NBPTS) is an independent, nonprofit organization founded in 1987 made up primarily of classroom teachers, but also includes school administrators, local and state school board members, governors and state legislators, education officials, and business and community leaders. They promote National Board Certification, a national voluntary system to assess and certify teachers who meet high and rigorous standards and to advance education reforms.

Professional Development

ADVANCEMENT
IN THE PROFESSION

Even though there are usually differences in the responsibilities of administrators and teachers, teachers and paraprofessionals, certified staff and classified (or noncertified) staff, the teaching profession is not one that makes many distinctions within its ranks. As classroom teachers, we don't get promotions like those typically offered in the business world, and often we feel there is little opportunity for advancement without leaving the classroom. With the proper credentials, adequate experience, and a willing attitude, however, teachers can increase both their earning power and their professional standing—most often by increasing their responsibilities—and have the choice of continuing successfully in the classroom or moving into another aspect of education.

Have a Professional Growth Plan

Know where you want to go and what you want to do as a teacher. Whether you choose to spend your career in the classroom or move into another phase at some point, be in charge of where you are and where you are going. Whether you must submit a professional growth statement to your school or not (most districts require them), you need to have a plan. To determine your professional growth, you need to set goals and take the necessary steps to reach them.

Set one goal that is reasonably attainable, one that is jointly developed and agreed upon, whether initiated by you or by your supervisor. The accomplishment of a goal results in a change in behavior and is not merely a completion of activities. This goal might range from improving your professional credentials to improving your classroom management style. It should have a relationship to your district or school goals as well as to your own personal growth needs. You should be able to state why this goal is important and how it relates to previous evaluations. You should be able to determine measurable and observable outcomes, describe activities and strategies as well as give a time line, and include necessary resources you will need. Finally, you should be able to show how you will measure (or show accomplishment of) your goal. Will you have earned a master's degree, enabling you to assume more or different responsibilities, or will you have fewer office referrals for student discipline?

Growth plans are continuous and ongoing through-out your teaching career and should be viewed as a valuable component to your overall effectiveness in the classroom. After submitting your professional growth plan to your administrator, keep a copy for your own records for purposes of review and continuity. Actually make it a part of your thinking, your planning, and your behavior—not just another paper hoop to jump through for the bureaucracy. It should be your action plan for success.

Check Your Teaching Certificate

Be sure your credentials are up-to-date and adequate for the areas in which you want to be involved. Most areas of teaching require specific types of certification; to move into counseling or administration, for exam-ple, requires additional course work and experience that will lead to the specialized certification. Pay atten-tion to renewal dates and be sure you have your coursework completed and your paperwork on file in plenty of time. Otherwise, you could find yourself unemployed until your certificate is in order and in the hands of the proper authorities. By law, you must keep your license current, and it must be on file with your personnel office. In most places, you won't be allowed to teach without it.

For specific requirements in your own state, check

with your school's personnel office; for information about other states, check the most recent edition of *Teacher Certification Requirements in All Fifty States, How and Where to Get a Teaching Certificate in All Fifty States,* listed in Appendix B.

For information on licensure laws, contact: PLACE Program, National Evaluation Systems, Inc., 30 Gatehouse Road, P.O. Box 660, Amherst, MA 01004-9009, Telephone: (413) 256-2885; telecommunications device for the deaf: (413) 256-8032.

Obtain Necessary Experience and Training

Whether you have an advanced degree or not, ongoing education is a must for the professional teacher. Staff development opportunities, conferences in specific discipline areas, and summer seminars, either for graduate credit or subject area enrichment, are all ways to enhance that degree and make your résumé more attractive.

Check out the staff development and in-service opportunities available in your district and in your area. School districts regularly send out information on classes and seminars being offered throughout the year. Do not throw these in the round file! Staff development classes are usually inexpensive, and even though the college credit may seem small, those individual units add up. If no credit is offered, the class may still be a valuable investment of your time. Most importantly, you will be keeping current and involved with your profession.

Stay on Top of Salary Increases

Teachers can enhance their basic salary primarily in two ways: through more education and through experience. Typically, advanced degrees and graduate level credits beyond the last degree earned will be worth the cost of the coursework. The investment you make in getting that advanced degree will pay off in increased salary every year you teach, just as every year you remain in a system will put you at a higher level on the salary schedule. You need the constant upgrading of skills not only for renewal of your teaching certification, but for its monetary value as well.

Apply for promotion on the salary schedule, such as lane changes or other categories for salary increases, as soon as you qualify. Keep track of credits earned through staff development and college classes. Have a file especially designated for these papers and be sure that you apply for advancement on the salary schedule. Otherwise, you are losing money unnecessarily!

Consider National Board Certification

The commitment required to complete National Board Certification is a big one, but it is a significant way to affirm your excellence and demonstrate your commitment to providing the finest teaching to your students. It offers an excellent opportunity for professional growth even though it is not mandatory and will continue to be a voluntary program. For more information, to get involved in national certification, or to request an application, call the National Center for Innovation at (202) 822-7350 or the National Board at 1-800-22TEACH.

Go to Those Conferences!
Subject area conferences and professional association conferences are both good places to increase your knowledge and enhance your repertoire of teaching skills and techniques, as well as make valuable contacts. The conference is one of the best places to pick up ideas for teaching, to buy new and useful materials, and to network with other professionals. Most beginning teachers, and many who have years of experience, cannot afford the registration fee, let alone the costs of travel, hotel accommodations, and food for a week or even a weekend. Conference costs vary widely and can often be quite expensive, but there are several ways to make them more affordable.

Most administrators have funds for professional development that can be used for this purpose. They will usually at least help defray the registration fees and often pay for part of the housing costs. If the conference is one that will address the goals of your school and/or the district's strategic plan, administrators are usually more willing, maybe even eager, to help you get there. You are not only enhancing your own professional skills, but promoting the goals of the school community as well. Pay attention to conference topics. Talk to your principal or curriculum specialist to find out how to request conference attendance, and do it!

Another good source for conference assistance is your professional association. Most organizations offer conferences for a wide variety of professional enrichment purposes. Don't assume that these offerings are out of reach or earmarked only for certain people. It's not just members of the executive board who get to go, and delegates usually are not expected to pay their own way. An active association wants broad member participation and will usually pay for members to attend these conferences. The association frequently will pick up most of the accompanying costs and occasionally even include some kind of stipend, depending upon the degree of involvement or commitment. Most often an election will be held to select representatives, but all you need to do is get your name on the ballot (usually by simply volunteering) and with a little bit of luck, you can be the one who gets paid to go, gets the training, and makes the contacts while having a great experience.

Take on Extra Responsibility at the Building Level

Teachers who want to assume a bit more responsibility almost always start by taking on the numerous tasks that are part of their own education community—in their own buildings. The degree of extra involvement depends on where you are in your career. Beginning teachers many times also have pressing family or social commitments in addition to the almost Herculean tasks of getting started—accumulating supplies, writing plans and developing materials from scratch, experimenting with every facet of classroom management—and so will choose not to take on more work until their other responsibilities have eased a bit. Nevertheless, many opportunities for extra challenge and stimulation (translate: work) abound, and with the added work comes opportunity to advance, both monetarily and professionally.

Definitions and perceptions of extra duty vary widely from district to district—indeed, sometimes from person to person. Nevertheless, the term generally applies to those duties not typically engaged in by the regular classroom teacher, such as the following.

Department leader: A department leader is typically responsible for interdepartment communication, collaborates with other teachers in the department, communicates with key administrators, and represents the department at building and district level meetings, works with the principal to interview prospective teachers, assigns teaching responsibilities, orders materials and establishes budgets, and schedules meetings. Department leaders are compensated in a variety of ways: Some schools allow an extra planning period and/or a percentage of the teacher's annual salary as pay for this extra responsibility. The terms of this compensation are usually spelled out in the negotiated agreement. Usually, this position is one either appointed by the principal or selected by the department members by a variety of methods: someone volunteers, the job rotates, the department holds a formal election—sometimes they even draw straws! Pay also varies from several hundred to several thousand dollars, depending on factors such as size of the department, seniority, determined responsibilities, and the negotiated salary schedule.

Team leader: Again, a team leader may be chosen by the principal or by the group—according to expertise, seniority, or degree of interest. Compensation is similar to that of a department leader, depending on the size of the team and the responsibilities of the team leader.

Coaching: Whether coaching athletics or speech, this is a time-honored method of supplementing a teacher's income. More and more schools are hiring coaches who specialize in a given sport or activity and who have no other teaching responsibilities or connections to the school. Most districts, however, still look first to teachers to fill these positions. The pay depends upon the length of the season and on the salary schedule but usually increases as the coach's experience increases. Many teachers look forward to coaching at least one, and sometimes several, extracurricular activities, because it not only helps supplement their income, but it is yet another way to reach young people and to work with them in another arena.

Yearbook/newspaper: Especially at the high school level where the complexity of the production of a weekly or monthly newspaper as well as of a professional, comprehensive yearbook is a major undertaking, this added responsibility is often inadequately funded, considering the number of hours invested in supervising students outside of class, conferencing with sales representatives, and negotiating coverage of every school activity all year long. Nevertheless, some compensation is to be expected and nearly always follows an established schedule. It is typically commensurate to that of coaches.

Dramatic productions: Frequently, drama and theater teachers, English teachers, and music teachers—either individually or in collaboration with other disciplines—take on the responsibility of producing student performances. Whether these are schoolwide or department-sponsored, there is almost always some extra pay involved due to the amount of extra time, preparation, and supervision required.

Class sponsor: Depending on the school district, taking on the responsibility of supervising students in their extracurricular student body and class activities can be one way of earning extra money. Many beginning teachers will volunteer this extra duty in order to become more knowledgeable and well-rounded; in other schools special activities directors are part of the faculty.

Club sponsor: This is one of those areas that usually falls to the special interests of a particular faculty member. From book discussion groups and academic honoraries to civic groups and antidrug coalitions, teachers find themselves involved in providing leadership for all kinds of worthwhile school and community groups, usually with no pay except the personal reward of working with students in a common area of interest. Some groups that are traditionally school-sponsored and sanctioned, however, such as the National Honor Society, occasionally come with some stipend attached for the faculty advisor.

Other methods: Music teachers often give private lessons, and some other teachers are also able to teach summer school and/or night classes, or tutor special classes after their regular work day.

Administrative Requirements

Teachers who want to move into another arena of education usually pursue advanced degrees or certification in administration. The requirements for the various positions available in a school system vary from district to district, but the most common include the following.

Principal: In most states, the principal must have a minimum of five years experience in the classroom and hold a certificate or license in public school administration. This individual is the education leader in the school building, responsible for personnel decisions, hiring and firing and supervision, budget, day-to-day operations, curriculum, instructional materials, organization management, program evaluation, and communication and progress reporting to the community.

Assistant principal: The qualifications for the position of assistant principal are the same as those for the principal, but without the actual practical experience in the position of principal. There may be one or several assistant principals depending upon the size of the school. This person is often seen as a "principal in training," but is technically the right arm to the principal, sharing the responsibilities of the principal, and often assuming responsibility for areas specially designated or agreed upon, such as discipline, student government, teacher evaluation, or athletics.

Superintendent: Having both classroom experience and holding a teaching certificate/license as well as credentials in school administration, the superintendent is the chief administrator of a school system, responsible for implementing the school board's policies, rules and regulations, and enforcing state and federal mandates, as well as representing the school district as its educational leader. There is a superintendent at the state level as well as in each local school district.

Assistant superintendent: Depending upon the size of the school district, there may be one or several assistant superintendents whose responsibilities complement those of the superintendent and whose job requirements are the same. They, too, will have had classroom experience and hold school administration certification. Often, in larger districts, an assistant superintendent may be in charge of one specific area such as the budget or secondary or elementary schools, or some other area of specialized expertise.

Curriculum specialist: The curriculum specialist for a district will most often have advanced training in a content area as well as experience in administration. The requirements and responsibilities vary from district to district, but they typically include coordinating the curriculum in a content area, such as math or English, throughout the grade levels. This person works as a resource for classroom teachers and facilitates districtwide communication and staff development for curriculum-related concerns.

Personnel director: The personnel director, whether for classified or certified employees, is in charge of all personnel policies and protocol including recruiting, arranging for interviews, record keeping, and human resources. As a human resource director, this individual will be qualified in areas of personnel development and will have advanced degrees in personnel or related fields.

Information systems director: This person is typically responsible for information storage and retrieval and works with the district computer system and oversees the purchase and use of computers, computer labs, and all other technological information systems. The qualifications for this position usually include expertise and advanced degrees in business and technology.

Organizational or staff development director: Responsible for organizing, coordinating, implementing, and evaluating staff development, this central administration staff person works with other administrators and curriculum specialists to provide professional growth opportunities to all employees in the district. Advanced training and/or experience in facilitating employee education and public school administration are necessary.

Media and technology support services director: As a media specialist, this person is in charge of all technological media for the district, providing instructional materials and equipment and technological support for school media centers and teachers. Besides teaching experience and library and media training and certification, this position requires administrative expertise as well.

Accountability and assessment director: Typically responsible for testing, assessment, and evaluation districtwide and for reporting state and federal requirements, the director of accountability and assessment works with other district personnel to develop, administer, and evaluate district assessments of standards in all content areas. This person must have actual classroom teaching experience, familiarity with the curriculum, and administrative skills.

Research and development director: This person is primarily responsible for facilitating educational research in the district, encouraging innovative programs, and providing assistance in acquiring financial and technical support for various educational programs throughout the district. The requirements for this position typically include skills in grant writing and communication, as well as teaching and curriculum development experience.

Become Involved at the District Level

Be alert to opportunities at the district level as well as at the building level for involvement in curriculum development and writing. Frequently, serving on instructional improvement committees and applying for support grants for innovative teaching or research methods and strategies will pay off in a variety of ways.

Extra pay for extra work: Many committee members (such as textbook selection committees, standards development committees, curriculum writing teams) are now paid for the time they put in after hours. Hourly rates vary widely from district to district and state to state.

Increased responsibility: Most school districts frequently utilize a "Teacher on Special Assignment" (TOSA) designation, allowing teachers to take on added responsibility for special projects or assignments. By becoming involved with district strategic goals and ongoing projects, teachers can become a vital part of their school community. Through committee work and proving their skills to the people in charge—plus making frequent and meaningful contact with administrators—people move into key positions. Work on committees, review boards, curriculum writing teams, test development projects, and other education-related professional activities can even lead to opportunities at state and national levels, if you are interested and have broadened your professional involvement beyond the classroom.

Financial and technical support: Grants and other forms of financial support are often available for individual educators as well as for schools and school districts. Businesses and other members of the community make financial contributions, volunteer in the schools and give technical support. Whether this assistance is achieved through formal channels—watch for programs advertised through school communications—or informally, pay attention to offers made in the most casual of settings. Don't hesitate to request help for specific needs from members of your community; they want to help, but you have to ask for it! Businesses will often provide computers, transportation, art materials, building supplies, books, mentors (a computer engineer mentoring a junior high student can forge a lifetime friendship and a priceless ally for both schools in general and for the individual student in particular), or needed funds for a special project. Often, programs are in place for businesses and individuals to channel their efforts and their support, but even without such formal sanction, there are many resources in every community. Become involved in your community so that you know what opportunities are available to both your students and yourself.

HOW TO GET A GOOD EVALUATION

Even though everyone must go through the evaluation process and we all know the criteria that must be met, some people invariably seem to have an inside track. What do they do that makes them look so good? They have the same qualifications on paper, have similar responsibilities, and perform at comparable (or even lower) levels; why, then, do they get such good end-of-the-year reviews? Besides doing their jobs well, what are they doing?

Be Self-Sufficient

First of all, these teachers have learned to meet most challenges by themselves. Before going to the office for a solution to a problem, enterprising, independent teachers will try to work it out themselves. Whether you need a field trip form, want to request a personal day, need to order a textbook or fax a document, have a complaint about another faculty member's loud classroom, or can't handle another sassy remark from another student or another whiny excuse from a parent, try to handle it yourself! Remember the good advice, "Don't ask others to do for you what you can do for yourself." It works. Naturally, we all have to ask for help occasionally, and you should not be afraid to ask for help if it's truly needed, but if those times are rare and only when absolutely necessary, the help will be much more willingly given and you will be viewed as someone who can and does take care of things.

In other words, don't go to the office and ask for

help finding something before you've even looked for it. Don't go running to the principal when you have a complaint about the teacher across the hall from you— talk to the teacher individually (and privately) first. Don't automatically send students to the office for every infraction—a missing pencil or an unexcused tardy does not warrant a trip to the office. If you bother the main office with little things, you will be seen as weak, incompetent, and petty, not busy, efficient, or strict! There will be times when you must send a student to the office for disciplinary action, when you can't work out a problem with a colleague or parent, or even when you really can't work the copy machine, and you will want to know that your request will be taken seriously and not brushed off. You don't want to be seen as a nuisance or incompetent.

Let's face it: Teachers are notoriously naive and idealistic—especially about office politics. We tend to believe that if we are dedicated to children and what's educationally best for them, everything will work out just the way it should. We want to believe that all parents are supportive, that other teachers share our priorities and philosophy, and that administrators are there to be our personal mentors, protectors, and saviors, if necessary. And then, we find ourselves in the principal's office, not with a misbehaving student, but in the presence of an angry parent or an upset colleague. Principals, no matter how supportive they are, do not want to have to bail you out very often. If you go running to your principal with many complaints, chances are it will show up on your evaluation—and not with

113

the observation that you were concerned, conscientious, or on top of things, either!

Remember that you are in charge of your own fate. You can help your principal see you in the most positive light or you can share your shortcomings with her. True, you will be asked what your areas of weaknesses are, but this is not the time to unburden your soul. If you confess that you still have problems with discipline and classroom management, this is exactly what will show up on your evaluation, whether the principal has observed this or not. Rather than point out these crucial areas that you may still need help with, mention one that, in the long run, can be seen as a strength—such as, "I need to work on finding time for myself."

Then, find a friend to help you with the area that has you most concerned: a critical friend, a teaching buddy. More and more schools are utilizing the mentor concept for teachers as well as for students, and it's about time. Having another teacher offer suggestions and support is much more reasonable and realistic than expecting an already overburdened administrator to be able to be available on a daily basis at the time that help is most needed. This is not to say that teachers should not look to their principals as educational leaders, but let's be honest: they cannot be responsible for the countless interactions that teachers face daily, and if we expect them to, we will diminish their effectiveness when we most need their intervention.

Share Your Successes

On the other hand, principals do need to be kept abreast of the big picture, of the successes of programs, student accomplishments, and your professional activities. Do not be afraid to share with administrators the good things that are happening in your classroom. Far too often, they are only involved with the problems and are not aware of what is going well for you. Tell them! Don't wait until formal evaluation time to sit down and pull out your list—invite your administrators into your classroom to see students working on projects and assignments throughout the year, as well as to take part in special events and performances. Let them know what your students are doing and ask them to come in and observe. These informal observations will make a lasting impression that will be far more favorable than the official observations scheduled for evaluation purposes (when you are probably nervous and uncharacteristically stiff).

Be aware that principals do not gather all their information through "official" channels. The office secretary, the custodian, other teachers, students, and parents all have influence over your evaluation. Pay attention to your interaction with them: Turn in your paperwork on time, straighten up your room before you leave at the end of the day, enforce all school rules, keep parents well informed, and work individually with 168 students every day, and you, too, should get a good report!

SUMMER "OFF"? NOT LIKELY

"You lucky teachers—you have the summer off." How many times have you heard this one? Well, many of us do have the summer free from classroom teaching duties, but this doesn't mean we get to spend that time lying in a hammock. This is the time that our other professional duties take priority, allowing us to be ready when fall and our students return. This is the time when we do our long-range planning and curriculum writing, when we take classes to strengthen our content knowledge and build our repertoire of teaching techniques and creative ideas. This is when we may even travel, write books, take part in dramatic or music performances, or paint pictures. Whatever enrichment we enjoy, rest assured it will be brought back into the classroom come September. So use the summer to get ready for the fall.

Check out what is available:

- staff development/curriculum writing
- summer classes/seminars
- graduate programs/institutes
- paid positions with the school district or in the community
- travel opportunities, domestic and foreign
- independent study grants and fellowships

Travel? On My Salary?
Teachers can travel, particularly if they are willing to get paid and/or earn college credit at the same time.

Opportunities to study and/or teach abroad are numerous, but require some searching out. Many opportunities involve a commitment of several months to a year or two and would require quitting or taking a leave of absence from current employment. Many, however, can be undertaken during a summer or other extended break. Teachers often take advantage of the breaks from the regular school year schedule, whether summer vacation, spring break, or winter intermission, to see the world—especially by sponsoring student trips to historical sites in their own country or to points of cultural interest in foreign lands.

Student trips: There are several different travel groups that will take you through the process step by step, from recruiting participants and informing parents, to arranging itineraries and travel accommodations, providing tour guides and security personnel, as well as taking responsibility for legal and financial obligations and arrangements. What may appear to be a lot of work can really pay off when your whole trip to Washington, D.C., or Paris, France, is completely paid for by the effort you put into it. You can take a handful of students or a huge group of two or three hundred people, complete with other teacher sponsors and any parents who either pay to go along as participants or who work as chaperones for part or all of the cost. For years, teachers have been taking students to Mexico or Germany or France for foreign language and cultural adventures, or to New York City or Rome or London for cultural exposure to art, music, and drama, and the more experience they get, the easier it gets to plan, organize, and execute the trips.

117

Many teachers not only experience fabulous trips for their own intellectual and cultural development, which they are able to incorporate into their class-rooms, but they are able as well to afford the travel expenses and even supplement their regular income by several hundred or even a thousand dollars, depending on how ambitious and energetic they are. The first step you need to take is to follow up on one of those offers in the many flyers that find their way into your mailbox. This approach is very attractive to those who not only like to travel for free, but who are also good at organiz-ing and who like traveling with groups—especially with kids. Be sure to check out potential agencies by contact-ing other teachers in your district who have used them. Find out the details of their programs and verify their reputability with people you know and trust. There are many reputable agencies to help you get started and carry through. Watch for their materials in the mail, use the Internet to find information, pick the brains of other teachers in the community who have tried this method of travel, and before you know it—bon voyage!

Besides student travel services, for information and assistance in planning you should check with NEA Advantage Travel Service for International Travel and Cruises. For a free copy of their international holiday and cruise brochures, call 1-800-811-9246.

Conventions and Conferences
If, after spending nine months with students, traveling with them during a holiday does not sound attractive, remember there are other ways to satisfy your wander-

lust. Take advantage of professional development opportunities that come your way. Attending conventions, particularly those sponsored by your professional association, provides excellent possibilities to serve your organization and get in some sight-seeing as well. All teachers' groups need delegates to attend state and national assemblies and many pay most, if not all, of the expenses for teachers who go. Many new teachers—even many who aren't so new—don't realize that they don't have to bear the expense of these trips themselves, and consequently don't consider them as real travel possibilities. Conventions are often held in some of the most beautiful and exciting cities in the world, but getting there and finding decent accommodations could be cost-prohibitive for most teachers. If the airfare and the hotel are free, however, or even greatly reduced, you too can visit some pretty exotic vacation spots while you are performing your professional duties. Yes, you will have to go to the meetings (which you will probably find educational and interesting, believe it or not), but your evenings and designated free time can be spent taking in the local attractions. The convention itself will provide lots of opportunities to attend concerts, go on guided tours of historical and scenic areas, see plays, watch sports events, and take in other vacation activities. The costs for these diversions will have to come out of your own pocket, of course, but they are usually less expensive because of the group rates you will get. Spouses are almost always welcome, but unless they are delegates, too, they will naturally have to pay their own way. Again, be alert to announcements regarding conventions that you would be interested in attending; you will benefit while working and the costs are minimal.

On a smaller scale, going to conferences is another excellent vehicle for travel. Within your discipline alone, you will find numerous conferences offered throughout the year, ranging from one- and two-day meetings to several days spent at some charming little getaway or at a big-city hotel. If conferences are not paid for out of your school's budget, there are other ways to cut expenses and still get to go. You can sometimes represent your subject area for the whole district and be reimbursed at the district level, if you agree to bring back what you learn and share it with your colleagues either at a staff meeting or through some other means of communication (such as an article for a staff newsletter, a building in-service program, or an area meeting). Contact your district resource coordinator, curriculum specialist, or staff development coordinator. Discuss the possibilities of such a plan and show your willingness to take on this responsibility. You will not only benefit your school district, but you will have a chance to get out of town, talk with other adults in your profession, and have a good time while you're at it.

With enough advance planning, you could also be a presenter at the conference itself. (See the section later in this chapter on how to be a successful presenter.) Frequently, a school district will be willing to take care of some or all of the travel and registration costs for teachers who are distinguishing themselves in this manner. Occasionally, the costs might be waived completely or offset by a stipend paid by the organizers of the conference. You will need to approach school administrators and/or conference organizers about this possibility. Talk to your department chair, principal, director, curriculum specialist, or superintendent; tell them what you're doing, explain how your presentation will benefit the department, school, or district, and ask for some financial support in the form of registration fees, travel, and hotel costs. It can't hurt to ask, and sometimes they say yes!

Again, you are going to have to work in order to get to travel this way—but you didn't expect to get something for nothing, did you? Seriously, even though you might not be able to run off to San Francisco for the weekend any time you feel the urge, with enough ambition and initiative, you can use your professional expertise instead of cash (or credit cards!) to pay your way. Naturally, to take advantage of these potential working/travel opportunities, you will need to be a member of the professional groups within your discipline and you will need to keep abreast of the current concerns in your particular area of education. You will have to respond to calls for presentations when those brochures hit your mailbox, and you will have to put forth some effort beforehand to prepare for your presentation. You will also spend a portion of your trip actually making your presentation—usually for about an hour in a small informal setting similar to a classroom. Depending on the popularity and relevance of your subject, the audience could range from three or four individuals to several hundred. Regardless of the size of your audience, however, the work and time that you invest will pay off, not only professionally, but personally. You will advance yourself and your skills professionally, and you will get to go places you might not have had the opportunity to visit otherwise.

Seminars and Institutes

If the idea of speaking before an audience does not appeal to you, you might want to consider attending seminars and institutes designed specifically for your subject or area of interest, where you can be involved as a participant rather than as a presenter. Again, some initial work must be expended in applying for acceptance to these programs, but if you will invest the time and energy necessary to submit a professional, quality application, your chances of being accepted are probably excellent. You have to spend some time and effort to prepare a well-written résumé and perhaps an essay discussing your academic interests and educational plans, but the payoff is well worth it.

Most seminars and institutes are group oriented with the major focus on a specialized area of study that appeals to educators in a common field with mutual interests in a specific topic. They will concentrate on very specific areas of study and can take you all over the world. Some programs include travel to relevant sites. These are typically aimed at enhancing the teacher's own intellectual development and cultural experience (which will in turn be brought back to enrich their students' studies) and often stimulate not only academic and professional growth, but many times provide outstanding travel opportunities as well. They nearly always pay a stipend to cover travel, living, materials, and tuition costs, and some even award enough to actually allow you to show a little profit for your efforts. The amounts vary considerably, depending upon the length of the seminar or institute, as well as its popularity and funding. They also give academic credit with a fairly wide range, too. Some may give only two or three semester hours of graduate credit, while others may be worth as much as nine hours. This credit is awarded in addition to the stipend.

The competition for acceptance in these institutes and seminars can be pretty vigorous, but most people don't even take the time to apply. You will need to keep your résumé up to date, so that you will have the necessary professional background information at your fingertips, and you will need to be able to write a decent essay, which is almost always required in the application. If you are not a good writer, after you get your basic ideas on paper, get someone to help you (like your good buddy in the English department!). Don't be timid about applying; even if you don't have a string of degrees and honors after your name, your desire and your reasons for attending the seminar are what will most qualify you.

Even though most of these classes are made up of large numbers of participants, some grants and fellowships are aimed at providing the opportunity for individual research and development and can be pursued at a self-guided pace. For example, if you have an idea for research that can be applied academically, you might be able to submit a proposal that will not only bring in the necessary funding required, but will allow you to travel and enrich your professional achievement, benefiting in turn both your school's department and your personal classroom effectiveness. You might obtain a grant that would pay enough to enable you to pursue a professional interest during the summer instead of having to get a second job just to make ends meet. (I submitted a proposal to the National Council for Basic Education a few years ago that allowed me to study during a six-week period, reading historical accounts, journals, novels, and literary criticism of the American Southwest. At the end of my reading I made several trips to visit historical monuments and cultural sites, all of which were paid for by the grant. As part of the grant, my school also received a substantial library award that allowed us to purchase books related to my study for the whole student body to enjoy.)

Most often, the philosophy of the funding agency or endowment is that support of the intellectual growth and development of teachers will ultimately benefit students. Through the materials, activities, and ideas that the teacher brings back to the classroom, the students' education is enhanced and enriched.

Continuing Education
All teachers know that they must continue to grow professionally and intellectually by continuing to be students themselves. Most teachers, not only because they want to, but also because their certification regulations require it, continue their education throughout their careers. This is accomplished most commonly through

summer coursework at colleges and universities, through seminars, institutes, individual study programs, and travel. Many of these educational opportunities can supplement the teacher's regular income as well as provide needed credit for recertification. Many offer a stipend (ranging from several hundred dollars to several thousand, depending on the length and workload of the study) as well as college credit.

They can also be tax deductible if there is a direct relationship to improving your classroom skills. The simplest way is to sign up for a credit course—an overseas tour or domestic travel program under the auspices of a college or university. Because the course is structured for a definite academic purpose, the IRS does not usually see a conflict between the professional and personal nature of the tour—as long as the course is related to your general teaching field. If your school district gives in-service credits for travel, you already have a strong case for a deduction. Just be sure to keep all receipts, registration forms, and notes on how the course/travel improved your skills. Not only are your travel and education expenses tax deductible, but any expenses for classroom exhibits and teaching supplies also qualify.

Lodging at university campuses provides easy access to dining and recreational facilities in stimulating and inviting surroundings where you can meet international travelers and enjoy the numerous cultural advantages that are part of a campus setting. Check with the *U.S. and Worldwide Teachers Travel Accommodations Guide* for rates, dates, activities available, phone numbers, addresses, reservations—all you need to know.

For more information about specific classes, contact colleges and universities for course catalogs. For more information about summer institutes or travel opportunities, watch for flyers or brochures that come through school mail, search out opportunities that might be available in the community or through professional associations, use the computer, and find information provided on the Internet by checking out educational listings and forums.

The Division of Education Programs of the National Endowment for the Humanities each year offers study opportunities for teachers and administrators. Full-time educators in public or private American schools are eligible to apply for summer seminars; participants will be awarded a stipend of $2,450, $2,825, or $3,200, depending upon the length of the seminar. Participants who teach in New Jersey are awarded an additional travel stipend by the Geraldine R. Dodge Foundation. Applicants should determine eligibility requirements by consulting seminar and institute directors individually. Topics and locations of seminars and institutes offered vary each year, so updated lists must be consulted annually. For information about NEH programs for schoolteachers and for current offerings, contact:

> The Division of Education Programs
> National Endowment for the Humanities
> 1100 Pennsylvania Ave. NW
> Washington, DC 20506
> Tel: (202) 606-8377
> (202) 606-8282 for the hearing-impaired only

Grants and Fellowships

Fellowships for independent study are available to qualified teachers. If you are a full-time teacher in grades K–12 in the United States with at least half of your schedule in the humanities, or a librarian, special education, English-as-a-Second-Language or a reading teacher, you are eligible. You also must be in at least your fifth year of full-time teaching and plan to teach the humanities at least five more years; and have not previously been awarded a CBE Fellowship for Independent Study in the Humanities. The term "humanities" refers to academic subjects such as history, literature, languages, religion, philosophy, and the history, theory, and criticism of the fine arts. It does not include mathematics, computer science, physical or natural sciences, psychology, or sociology. The Council for Basic Education welcomes inquiries from teachers who are unsure of their eligibility. The number of fellowships awarded each year varies, but 175 to 200 is typical. For complete information and application forms, contact:

> National Council for Basic Education
> 725 Fifteenth Street, NW
> Washington, DC 20005
> Tel: (202) 347-4171
> Fax: (202) 347-5047

Principals are also eligible to apply under a separate program. Requests for principal applications should be sent to:

> National Council for Basic Education
> Attn: 93PG
> P.O. Box 135
> Ashton, MD 20861

127

Grant and fellowship opportunities for teachers in every discipline are also provided by the Council for Basic Education Network of Fellows. This is an impressive offering of hundreds of awards, grants, fellowships, institutes, seminars, and independent studies with a wide range of financial support. The Council offers a booklet that lists all the opportunities in alphabetical order and includes the sponsor's name, address, and telephone number where available. These are followed by a brief description of the type of grant or funding offered and any application restrictions. An index arranged by deadline dates for application is also included. To obtain a copy of *Grant and Fellowship Opportunities for Teachers,* contact:

> Council for Basic Education
> Network of Fellows
> 1319 F Street, NW, Suite 900
> Washington, DC 20004-1152
> Tel: (202) 347-4171

Opportunities for Teaching Abroad

Opportunities to research, study, and/or teach abroad are numerous. Depending on one's interest, expertise, and flexibility, there are excellent opportunities to travel and to work and live in other countries. Often, educators are able to exchange teaching assignments, homes, and lifestyles for a school term. For specific information and application requirements, contact the institutions listed below:

American and Foreign Teachers
    Exchange Program
Office of Academic Programs
United States Information Agency (USIA)
301 Fourth Street, SW, Room 353
Washington, DC 20547
Tel: (202) 619-4555

Arranges one- and two-way exchanges of U.S. and foreign teachers, and summer seminars for U.S. teachers to study abroad.

American Educators Teaching Abroad
Superintendent of Documents
Government Printing Office
Washington, DC 20402
Tel: (202) 512-1800
Fax: (202) 512-2250

Bilingual Education
Rudolph Munis
Office of Bilingual Education and Minority
    Languages Affairs
U.S. Department of Education
220 C Street, SW, Room 5086
Washington, DC 20202
Tel: (202) 205-9700

Educational Exchange—University Lecturers (Professors) and Research Scholars (Fulbright-Hays Program)

Council for International Exchange of Scholars
3007 Tilden Street, NW, Suite 5M
Washington, DC 20008

Grants are awarded to improve and strengthen the international relations of the United States by promoting mutual understanding among the peoples of the world through educational exchanges.

Fulbright Foreign Policy Scholarships
Office of Academic Programs
600 Maryland Ave., SW
Washington, DC 20024

About five thousand grants are awarded each year to American students, teachers, and scholars to work abroad and to foreign citizens to teach, study, and conduct research in the United States. Contact this office for more information and application forms for the Fulbright program.

Fulbright-Hays Seminars Abroad—
Special Bilateral Projects (Fulbright Exchange)
International Studies Branch
Center for International Education
U.S. Department of Education
600 Independence Ave., SW
Washington, DC 20202
Tel.: (202) 401-9798

Grants for participation in short-term study seminars are awarded to qualified U.S. educators to increase mutual understanding and knowledge between the people of the United States and those in other countries.

Fulbright Memorial Program
Office of Academic Programs
600 Maryland Ave., SW
Washington, DC 20024

American teachers and education administrators can work in Japan under the auspices of the Japan-U.S. Educational Commission.

> Fulbright Teacher Exchange Program
> Office of Academic Programs
> 600 Maryland Ave., SW
> Washington, DC 20024

Opportunities are available for elementary and secondary school teachers and administrators and college faculty to attend seminars or teach in schools abroad. Grants in most cases include round-trip transportation. Applications must be submitted by October 15 for the following summer or academic year's program. Contact the Office of Academic Programs for information and applications.

For information on the International Educator Exchange Program, contact the Federal and State Program Services, located in your own State Department of Education, or contact:

> International Education Exchange
> Office of Educational Research and Improvement
> U.S. Department of Education
> Washington, DC 20208
> Tel: (202) 219-2079

These grants are awarded to support international education exchange activities between the United States and eligible countries in civics, government, education, and economics.

For assistance in foreign travel that does not involve a

131

formal program or grant award, several agencies would be helpful. One specifically geared toward educators is the private travel network of B & B's for educators:

Educators Bed and Breakfast Network
Box 5279, Eugene, OR 97405
Tel: 1-800-377-3480
Fax: (541) 686-5818
Home page: http:/ / www.efn.org/edbabnet

An outstanding source book for all kinds of grants, awards, and other types of assistance (both monetary and technical) for schools and educators in every field is *Lesko's Info-Power*. This book is a gold mine of information on where to get money and information for every need imaginable. Check it out—for your district, your school, your students, your family, your friends, yourself! It is listed in Appendix B.

CONSULTING/SPEAKING/PRESENTING

Consulting for and speaking at educators' meetings, conferences, and conventions is an excellent way to become known, to increase your income, and to advance professionally. Most teachers don't look at the world beyond the classroom as being their arena for demonstrating their expertise; however, sharing what you do well and what you know best is important to other teachers and the wider community, as well as to your students. Consider what you do well and what you know a lot about: is it motivating students, teaching a specific skill or concept, organizing some aspect of the classroom or curriculum? Have you developed a program or teaching tool that others could use or adapt? What do other teachers ask you how to do? What teaching experiences have you had that are different? What methods or materials have you adapted in new ways?

If you have successful ideas that you have tried in the classroom recently and you are willing to share those ideas and methods with others, you should consider consulting. You are a practitioner and you know what works. Other teachers are looking for ideas and methods that have been tried. Consulting is fun, even though it is hard work, and it can benefit you as much as it helps others.

You Can Learn to Be a Presenter
Involvement in the wider education community can often lead to opportunities at the state or national level. Contacts made at conferences, in seminars, and working on committees can lead to leadership roles in speaking and presenting your own ideas, work, and expertise.

Watch for staff development opportunities for potential leaders in your district. Most teachers are not aware of the training opportunities available to them, because these help sessions or short seminars are most frequently targeted for administrators. However, teachers who want to learn to be more effective presenters for large conferences and even local or building meetings can profit by signing up for these courses. You will be taught how to organize your material more effectively, how to design and produce professional visual aids, and how to make your presentation in a more powerful manner.

Popular topics: Know what topics are in demand, such as the following.

- classroom management ideas
- uses for the classroom computer
- discipline techniques
- innovative ideas for teaching the basics
- curriculum writing
- crisis, loss, and conflict resolution
- teaching writing (both expository and technical)
- working with adolescents
- professional growth
- make/take workshops

Planning and outlining: To plan your presentation, write objectives for each section.

- What will teachers be able to do after they have participated in this workshop?
- What materials will they have to take back to the classroom?
- What new theories and ideas will teachers have as a result of this workshop?
- What different attitudes will they have?

Then, outline each section. List specific information/ideas as you will present them.

The intro: Write a strong introduction—one with "pizzazz." Get the audience interested immediately— use startling facts, impressive statistics, pertinent quotes, rhetorical questions, and related anecdotes to capture your listeners' interest. Focus their attention. Be sure that participants know what to expect and what helpful information, strategies, and techniques they can anticipate learning.

Conclusion: Write a conclusion that either challenges the listeners, tugs at their heartstrings, or makes them feel good about themselves.

Be sure to summarize main points, stress the primary focus of the presentation, and make a strong ending. A useful technique is to refer to some aspect of your introduction—reiterate the same facts, quotes, anecdotes, or questions you raised at the beginning. It will help ensure a cohesive presentation—one that "hangs together."

Plan the time span: Divide your presentation or workshop into segments that can be separated into one-and-a-half to two-hour sessions. Include :

- a short introduction of about 5 to 10 minutes about yourself, your professional background, and your philosophy.
- the last 10 minutes for closing.
- time for evaluation and feedback from participants.
- time for breaks.
- adequate time for lunch.
- ALWAYS START AND END ON TIME!

Prepare your presentation:
Prepare a packet of easily reproduced materials.
Either organize your materials and handouts into a packet yourself and charge for it, or send copy-ready

materials to the district to reproduce and collate. Include materials from overheads in the packet so your audience will not have to take copious notes as you talk, instead of listening to you.

Make overhead transparencies of your presentation.

- Talk from transparencies, not notes on paper.
- Invest in good quality transparencies if you will use them many times.
- Do not use small type for transparencies.
- Use colored transparencies and clear visual aids such as arrows, lines, and boxes to organize your ideas and topics that help you and your audience keep track of where you are.
- Make duplicates of your transparencies in case your originals get lost or damaged.
- Keep your transparencies in labeled folders to match your presentations.

Keep material organized in a briefcase so that you will have it ready for presentations.

- If you have more than one presentation, put them in separate cases.
- If you have books and displays, invest in a sales case.
- If you have many materials, invest in light-weight trunks.
- Buy cheap luggage on sale to keep books in to carry easily, especially on airplanes (where the luggage may be scratched or lost).

Continue to Polish Your Presentation

Keep abreast of and utilize technological advances. Transparencies can be updated and polished with colorful new layouts and sharp graphics generated by computers; they may even be replaced by improved technology that hasn't yet been made available to most budget-strapped educators. Whatever your topic, your workshop or seminar should be as professional and polished as you can make it; be sure you stay current with the trends in technology and use all available media to enhance your presentation. Other tips on polishing your presentation:

- Practice, practice, practice! Practice on videotape . . . in front of a mirror . . . on friends and colleagues.
- Submit proposals for conferences.
- Talk to college classes.
- Give in-service programs for your own department, grade level, or building.
- Volunteer to give programs in the district.
- Speak for libraries, service organizations, parents, and citizen groups.
- Consider joining a professional speaker's bureau for expanded exposure.

What Should You Charge?

Consider whether you will have to be absent from your regular job assignment, travel time, hotel costs, preparation time involved, and how well you are known professionally.

Standard fees begin at $200 per day, plus mileage or travel expenses, and per diem if you must eat meals or spend the night. Adjust your fees if you aren't well known and you need the exposure, and increase your fees as you work more often, especially if you lose salary to do the presentation or if it causes you undue hardship. Be sure to keep track of your expenses to see if you can afford to consult.

FINANCES

Teachers are not in the profession for the money, obviously. Nevertheless, we do need to make money in order to survive. Unless you are independently wealthy or have won the lottery, you will need to pay close attention to your financial situation. Even though most career teachers don't really have a great desire to be rich (if they did, they would go into a more lucrative field), they would like to be able to live without worrying about how they are going to make it to the next paycheck. This may not seem possible when you first begin teaching, especially if you have a family to support. However, with careful planning, realistic goals, and modest spending habits, you too can eke out a spartan existence!

Pay Attention to Your Paycheck
First, know how much you make. Take a good look at your salary schedule. See how much you're supposed to be making and if your check coincides with that

amount. Then carefully look over your pay stub. Be sure that you are withholding the proper amounts and that you are being paid what you were contracted for. Double-check the figures and make sure you understand how amounts are determined. Don't rely on the payroll department to catch all mistakes or, even worse, depend on them to never make mistakes. Your paycheck is your responsibility, no one else's.

Pay special attention to your pay stub. Check to see if payroll is withholding only what is necessary and what is to your benefit. Are you claiming too many dependents? Too few? Are you adequately covered through the district's group health plan, or could you do better through an independent plan or under a spouse's coverage? Do you have a long-term savings plan, an individual retirement account, or other tax-deductible savings opportunity you could take advantage of? Seek your tax accountant's advice.

Expense Worksheet
There are numerous tax guides on the market written specifically for teachers. The following expense worksheet and explanations are very basic and will only serve to get you started. For detailed information, consult a tax expert or a tax manual for teachers.

FIGURE 5-1
TEACHER'S EXPENSES
_____

SCHOOL   _____

SUBJECT/GRADE TAUGHT   _____

A. PROFESSIONAL FEES & DUES:

    Association Dues, Local   _____

    Association Dues, National _____

    Association Dues, Other   _____

    License and Credentials   _____

    PTA/PTO Dues   _____

B. EDUCATION EXPENSES:

    Note: If either question below is NO, then deduction not
    allowed:

    1. Were you meeting employer requirements for keeping
    your salary, status, or job?

    _____ yes _____ no

    2. Were you maintaining or improving skills required in
    your employment?

    _____ yes _____ no

List the courses you took:

_____

_____

_____

_____

Clerical, Typing Service (reports, questionnaires)   _____

Conferences, Seminars, Registration _____

Laboratory Fees, Research Fees _____

Student Body Card, Parking Permit _____

Textbooks, Supplies, Photocopies _____

Tuition, Correspondence Courses _____

Tutors/Transcripts _____

C. TELEPHONE EXPENSES:

Answering Machine or Service _____

Beeper or Pager _____

Cellular Phone _____

Fax Machine Messages _____

Home Telephone (business use) _____

Second Home Telephone (business use) _____

Office Long Distance _____

Outside Pay Telephone _____

Other _____

D. TOOLS, EQUIPMENT, AND SUPPLIES:

Admissions to Classroom-Related Activities _____

Art Shows, Artist Series _____

Concerts, Films _____

School Functions/Student Activities _____

Books, Recordings, Discs _____

Magazines, Newspapers _____

Supplies _____

Equipment (cost or repair) _____

Calculator, Typewriter, Computer _____

Camera, Film, Projector, Videotapes _____

Musical Instruments, Stereo _____

Desk, Chair, File Cabinet, etc. _____

Gifts and Treats _____

Prizes, Awards,Trophies _____

Postage, Printing, Photocopying _____

Payments to Substitute Teacher or Aide _____

Writing and Publishing Expenses _____

Safety Equipment _____

E. UNIFORMS AND UPKEEP:

Athletic Wear _____

Caps and Gowns _____

Laboratory Coat _____

F. BUSINESS MILES:

Chaperone at Events _____

Committee Meetings _____

Continuing Education _____

Field Trips, PTA/PTO/PAB Meetings _____

Mileage to Second Job (if on the same day) _____

Speaking Engagements _____

Student Home Visits _____

Total Business Miles _____

Total Miles Driven During the Year _____

Average Daily Round-Trip Commute _____

Total Commuting Miles for the Year _____

Parking Fees, Tolls _____

Train, Bus, Taxi, etc. (not overnight) _____

Date Car Placed in Service (MMDDYY) _____

G. OVERNIGHT TRAVEL EXPENSES:

Plane, Train, Bus, Subway _____

Car Rental, Tax Fees, Tolls, Parking _____

Motel _____

Telephone _____

Baggage, Laundry, Cleaning, Tips _____

Other _____

    Total Overnight Travel Expense   _____

    Reimbursement not on W-2 _____

H. MEALS AND ENTERTAINMENT:

Meals and Entertainment Expense @ $28/day   _____

Reimbursement not on W-2 _____

Total Teacher's Expense: _____

Is this form for Filer or Spouse?   F   S

Do you/your spouse have another vehicle for personal use?

                                                   Y   N

Is employer vehicle available for off-duty personal use?

                                                   Y   N

Do you/your spouse have evidence to support your deductions?

                                                   Y   N

If "Yes" is the evidence written?   Y   N

**Explanation of Tax Deductions
for Professionals***

A. Professional fees and dues: The deduction for business-related social or country club dues has been eliminated. Dues paid to professional organizations, labor unions, civic or public service organizations, business leagues, trade associations, chambers of commerce, boards of trade, and real estate boards will continue to be deductible as an ordinary and necessary business expense provided that a principal purpose of the organization is NOT entertainment.

B. Education expenses: The education must be required by your employer or the law: (1) to keep your present salary, status, job, or rate of pay, and serve a business purpose of your employer; or (2) to maintain or improve skills needed in your present position. You may be able to deduct the costs of qualifying education even though the education may lead to a degree. It is not qualifying education if it is needed to meet the minimal educational requirements of your present job, or will qualify you for a new trade or business.

C. Telephone expenses: You cannot deduct the cost of basic local telephone service, including taxes, for the first telephone line you have in your home. Long distance calls from the first telephone line are deductible, however, if the calls are business-related. The cost of a second telephone line is deductible if used only for business. The purchase cost of a cellular phone or fax

* *Source: Garland Lumbard, Lumbard's Income Tax, Accounting/ Audit Service (printed with permission).*

machine should be listed in Section D., equipment pur-
chases. The operating costs or monthly expenses should
be listed on the appropriate lines of Section C.

D. Tools, equipment, and supplies: To be deductible, the
expense must be both ordinary and necessary in your
business. An ordinary expense is one that is common
and accepted in your business. A necessary expense is
one that is helpful and appropriate for your business.
Generally, an expense for a tool or supply is deductible
in the year of purchase, if the tool or supply is used up
or worn out within one year from the date of purchase.

E. Uniforms and upkeep: The costs and maintenance of
uniforms and work clothes are fully deductible if: (1)
the uniforms are required by your employer (if you are
an employee); and (2) the clothes are not adaptable to
ordinary street wear. Usually, the employer's emblem
attached to the clothing indicates it is a uniform.

F. Business miles: Deductible car expenses include
those necessary to drive and maintain a car that you use
to go from one workplace to another in the same day.
This may include visiting customers or attending meetings away from your regular workplace, or between
your home and a temporary work location. This does
NOT include commuting from your home to a regular
work location. Record your date, destination, business
purpose, business miles, and car expense in a log book.

G. Overnight travel expenses: You are traveling away
from home if (1) you are out of your regular work location area longer than an ordinary day's work, and (2)
you need to sleep or rest while away from home. Keep
a written record of expenses for public transportation,

145

total miles driven, meals, lodging, telephone, baggage and shipping, laundry, cleaning, and tips. You may choose to use the standard meal allowance of $28 per day instead of keeping the actual expense receipts, but you must still keep records to prove time, place, and business purpose of your travel.

H. Meals and entertainment expenses: The deduction for the cost of meals and lodging while away from home on business is limited to amounts that are not lavish nor extravagant under the circumstances. A taxpayer must be able to prove that the expenses were in fact paid or incurred. The expenses must be substantiated as to (1) amount, (2) time and place, and (3) business purpose. A taxpayer always has the option of keeping the actual records or may use the per diem allowances of $28 per day for meals only, or $95 per day for meals, lodging, and incidentals.

Budget

Why budget? Many teachers will say, "I make so little that after the bills are paid, there's nothing left to budget with!" The answer is: Do it anyway. It's good practice for when you start making enough to live on. You need to understand your current financial situation—you need to know where your money is going and have a plan for using it rather than letting it just disappear. Set aside something for savings first, then determine how much you can allot for the major living expenses, such as housing, utilities, food, insurance, and fixed monthly payments.

Avoid credit cards! They become crutches for many people, rendering them helpless and dependent, rather than functioning as a tool to be used effectively. If you can pay off the balance every month, then a credit card is a valuable tool; if you find yourself using it to help you get to the end of the month and the balance continues to grow larger, then you're hurting yourself in the long run. Paying the exorbitant interest that credit card companies often charge just to be able to make monthly payments will put you in a financial hole you will find it very difficult to get out of.

Establish realistic goals and then formulate a strategy for financial success, just like you do for anything else. Evaluate investments objectively by doing a little research and then take action. Your financial stability is just as important as any other aspect of your life for which you are held accountable.

Be sure to sit down with a good financial adviser. Banks and credit unions have loan officers or "personal bankers" who will be glad to help you set up a workable budget. These financial experts can be invaluable when it comes to giving excellent financial advice and helping you set up a reasonable budget on which you can live.

FIGURE 5-2
SAMPLE BUDGET

INCOME:

    monthly take-home salary   _____

    income from other sources   _____

SAVINGS:

    savings accounts _____

    IRA accounts   _____

    tax-sheltered annuities _____

    retirement funds _____

    other   _____

INSURANCE:

    life   _____

    health   _____

    home   _____

    other   _____

CHARITABLE CONTRIBUTIONS:

_____

_____

_____

_____

LIVING EXPENSES:

    Monthly mortgage payment or rent   _____

Utilities:

electricity _____

gas _____

water _____

telephone _____

television cable _____

computer network _____

trash hauling service _____

lawn service _____

house repair/maintenance _____

cleaning (house) _____

laundry and dry cleaning _____

Food:

at home _____

carry-out/fast food _____

school lunches _____

business lunches _____

restaurant entertainment _____

Automobile Expenses:

insurance _____

taxes, registration, licenses _____

gasoline _____

oil _____

maintenance _____

repairs _____

Loans (other than mortgage):

    student loans _____

    car loans _____

    bank loans _____

    personal loans _____

Child care:

    day care _____

    lessons/tutoring _____

    babysitting expenses _____

      (for special occasions)

    child support _____

Medical expenses (not covered by insurance):

    doctor _____

    dentist _____

    other specialists _____

    prescriptions _____

Credit cards:

    _____

    _____

Clothing _____

Entertainment _____

Subscriptions:

    book clubs _____

    newspapers _____

    magazines _____

    other _____

Organization dues:

    professional associations _____

    civic organizations _____

    children's groups _____

Educational Expenses:

    tuition for classes _____

    books/materials/supplies _____

Special Classroom Supplies _____

Gifts:

    birthdays _____

    anniversaries _____

    holidays _____

    special occasions _____

Vacations and holidays _____

Miscellaneous expenses _____

Total monthly expenses _____

Remember: Plan your expenses
and don't spend money on anything that is not in your budget!

Ways to Supplement Your Income

Next, figure out how you can increase your salary. More education, more degrees, and more years in the same school system will enhance your earning power. It does pay to take additional coursework and to become more qualified, not only for the immediate placement on the salary schedule, but for the duration of your career. Throughout your career, your additional training will continue to add to your salary. Besides adding to your qualifications, you can make more money by adding to your responsibilities—by taking on more work.

Look for opportunities to make money for school-related activities:

Coaching: Depending on the sport or activity (such as speech, science, programs for gifted and talented students, or other special academically related activities), coaches can sometimes add significantly to their regular salary. Coaching is both time-consuming and energy-draining, but the payoffs are usually more than monetary. Whether one is working with young people in the classroom, on the basketball court, or in the performing arts, the involvement with students in another setting is both challenging and rewarding. Besides, many teachers have been hired because not only were they qualified in their subject area, they were willing and able to take on coaching responsibilities. In addition, with every year's experience the compensation normally increases somewhat.

Sponsoring extracurricular activities: These include the yearbook and school newspaper, class councils and student body councils, special student clubs, organizations and activities, directing dramatic productions—typically paid positions, even though the pay may be a pittance. Most teachers take on these jobs because "somebody has to do it," but keep in mind that some compensation goes with the task.

Most extra activities are available at the time contracts are signed, and you can ask for them, even if they are not initially offered. The range for most of these professional responsibilities is from $500 to $3,000 or $4,000 per year. An open, frank conversation with your principal or other district personnel about your financial needs can often lead to opportunities you might not have been aware of.

Department leadership: Another method of increasing your salary, especially after a few years of experience, is to become department chair or team or level leader. Again, the compensation may be somewhat meager, but these are paid positions and the compensation increases with experience. The responsibilities that are required of these leaders vary, but typically include curriculum coordination, department or grade level communication, communication with administrators and support services, and materials and supplies maintenance. Some schools give release time for carrying out such administrative duties; others give additional pay; some allow for both.

Summer school: It is most often taught by teachers who are willing to extend their teaching responsibilities through the summer. Many districts make available the opportunity for teachers to offer courses they would like to teach, either from the regular curriculum or as enrichment courses. These classes typically last for six weeks and may extend to a second six-week session, and the pay is most often comparable to a six-week employment compensation. Watch for announcements from the main administration offices, or contact the person in charge of summer school and curriculum early in the spring; even February is not too early to begin laying the groundwork for summer employment.

Night school and adult ed: Many teachers supplement their income by teaching night school, either for the school district, a community college, or continuing education courses offered by local colleges or universities. If you still have energy and time after spending a full day at your regular teaching job, teaching at night may be your answer to increasing your finances.

Adult education classes through your district or community college are often attractive alternatives for many teachers who would enjoy teaching older students at a more advanced level. Again, if time and energy permit, contact your local community college for teaching opportunities.

Other opportunities: In your district, they often include curriculum writing, workshops related to your district's strategies and goals, and committee work for special projects. The way to know about these is to be involved with what is going on in your school community. Serve on committees, attend task force meetings, and volunteer for extra responsibilities. One job leads to another as you network with other professionals in your area, and the effort will usually pay off!

Become involved with your professional association.

More often than not, this is the group that helps negotiate your salary, and you should inform yourself on the issues that determine how much and under what conditions you will be paid. Even if you dislike the political atmosphere of such activities, being concerned with matters that directly affect you is both necessary and responsible. The more you know, the more influence you can have. Offer to serve on negotiating committees and budget committees; volunteer to be an association representative from your building; pay attention to what is happening outside your classroom. These are areas that will directly impact your livelihood and your effectiveness as a professional educator.

Take Care of Yourself

(both professionally and personally)

Teachers are the epitome of the "giving" professions. We give of ourselves intellectually and emotionally. We give our knowledge (and our wisdom); we give our time (and our money); we give our energy; and we give our love. Over the years, we have given to the point of near exhaustion. We have taken on roles previously assumed by the community: parents, churches, neighbors, social agencies. These are "the whole village" used to assist in the education of our young people, but nowadays it seems teachers and schools are expected to do it all. We sponsor recreational activities for students on the weekends, help teenagers get jobs, and even provide childcare after school, as well as impart knowledge in the classroom. We teach not only English and math, but respect and manners. We feed not only our students' minds, but we make sure their nutritional needs are being met. We comfort, counsel, and assist them when they are hurt, rejected, neglected, abused, pregnant, addicted, convicted, and scared, and at the same time, we teach them to read and write. And we do it year after year with hundreds and hundreds of increasingly needy young people. We give until it would seem there is nothing left to give, and then we dig a little deeper and give some more. No wonder some teachers give up.

There are ways, though, to prevent giving up or burning out. We don't have to take on the weight of the world; we don't have to do it all. Let's learn to share . . .

Find a friend on the faculty: You can share ideas, give suggestions, provide encouragement, and be a critical friend (someone who offers honest, constructive criticism and supportive, friendly suggestions). Make friends with the other adults in your building. It's easy to become isolated, and isolation is a teacher's greatest underminer of confidence. Don't overlook the importance of being on good terms with the support staff in your building as well as with other teachers. Secretaries are a vital connection to getting things done and cutting through red tape. The custodial staff can help make your job considerably easier or more difficult, depending on your relationship with them. Treat them with the respect they deserve and they will be some of your greatest allies.

Find a fresh approach: This is essential to teaching a familiar idea or subject. You will teach the same thing year after year, and you will need a change of pace to remain fresh and enthusiastic about the material. The students will always be new each year, but if you try to teach exactly the same way every year, you will get bored and consequently you will bore your students.

Prioritize the demands on your time: Become a slave to your dayplanner and write down everything you must do. Your students, of course, will come first during the day, but even then, there are times when a counselor or administrator can better deal with a student's problems than you can. Learn early on that you cannot do it all, that education is a team effort. Involve the other professionals in your building and the students' parents. Make lists, keep notes, handle paperwork only once if at all possible, don't procrastinate, be flexible, and learn to say "no."

Delegate responsibility and build class identity: Encourage a team spirit and allow students to be responsible for their own education. Have them select (or you assign) study buddies to take notes and collect handouts for absent classmates and to help them catch up on missed classroom time.

Involve parents: Give assignments that include parent input; ask parents to chaperone trips, parties, and other class functions, to help out in the classroom, to be guest speakers, to serve on panels; make frequent phone calls to parents to ask for their opinion, advice, or to simply brag about their kid! Let parents know you value them as well as their child.

Join a community group: Be part of the larger community. You are the best spokesperson there is for education and people need to see you in the community as much as you need to have a life outside the classroom.

Join your professional organization: The support you will find among other professionals, the camaraderie, and the benefits of belonging to professional groups will far surpass the dues you will have to pay.

Let people know all the good things that are happening in your room: Invite the local news people in for special events and human interest story opportunities. Students deserve community attention and recognition for their achievements and activities.

Get in the habit of keeping good records: Use the computer whenever possible — put your grades, lesson plans, activities, parent contacts, discipline referrals, accident reports, and warehouse orders on discs. It will save you time in the long run, provide accountability, and keep you organized.

Remember to smile: Sometimes we take our jobs so seriously that we forget how much fun we can have. When teaching ceases to be fun, the teacher ceases to be effective.

Relax: Remember to take care of yourself. Set aside time to be good to you!

STRESS BUSTERS FOR TEACHERS

Teachers typically spend so much time and energy providing for other people's needs that they often forget to take care of themselves. The ones who are the best at paying attention to their students are frequently the same ones who neglect themselves. Consequently, they sometimes become victims of stress overload. To prevent stress and its common companion, burnout, learn to take good care of yourself first, so that you can continue to be there for your students and for your family, too.

1. Learn to recognize the symptoms.
- Listen to yourself.
- Pay attention to your body's signals.
- Recognize your needs.
- Avoid situations that you know upset you.

2. Give yourself a break.
- Take a walk.
- Look at the sky.
- Work out.
- Take a bubble bath.
- Daydream.
- Read a book for fun.
- Tune out the "news" . . . turn off the television and radio; skip the front page of the newspaper and go directly to the comics.

3. Find someone to talk to.
- Call a friend.
- Go out for coffee with a colleague.
- Visit a neighbor.
- Write a letter.
- Keep a journal.
- Give yourself a pep talk.

4. Be realistic.
- Set goals.
- Dream.

- Take on bite-size tasks.
- Do your best, but allow yourself to make mistakes.

5. Set priorities.
- Put yourself first sometimes.
- Ask yourself, "Will this decision make any difference twenty (or a hundred) years from now?"

6. Give yourself permission to say no.
- Make no apologies; just say no.
- Practice saying, "I must say no."

7. Get a good night's sleep.
- Wind down.
- Take a warm bath.
- Read something mindless.
- Play some soothing music.
- Drink some warm milk or nighttime herbal tea.

8. Spend time on yourself.
- Indulge in a hobby.
- Do your nails.
- Get a massage.
- Go window shopping.
- Go for a bike ride.
- Play a game.
- Lie in a hammock and fantasize.

9. Play with a baby.
- Get down on the floor and roll a ball.
- Make silly faces.
- Talk baby talk.

10. Pray. Meditate. Get in touch with your spirit.
- Listen to the wind blow.
- Watch the clouds.
- Go to a place of worship when no services are scheduled and let your soul be at peace.

The Teacher's Jargon

UNDERSTAND THE LANGUAGE

Regardless of the profession, discipline, or area of expertise, every job has its own language. Sometimes teachers use terms they have heard for years, having a vague understanding of their meaning, but not knowing the exact definitions or origins. They know they are going to an "IIC meeting" and what to expect there, but can't tell a newcomer what "IIC" stands for (Instructional Improvement Committee—at least, in some school districts). Buzzwords, of course, come and go with the current trends in education just as they do in any profession or aspect of our modern world. As concepts become widely accepted or go out of favor, our vocabulary constantly changes. What was the most popularly tossed about phrase last year may be the term to avoid today. Even though educational jargon is no substitute for clarity, knowing the commonly accepted terminology, understanding the "educatorese," and being able to communicate clearly with other professionals and the broader community are necessary skills.

The following glossary is by no means all-inclusive; the terms included here are ones that are commonly used by general classroom teachers and administrators, rather than by specialists. The definitions are, therefore, basic and broad, rather than detailed or narrow in scope. For in-depth discussion of any of the concepts, please research the current literature on the topic. These simple definitions are for quick, easy reference and basic clarification.

TERMS TO KNOW

ability grouping: the placement of students according to similar levels of intelligence or achievement in some skill or subject, either within or among classes or schools; tracking; homogeneous grouping.

abstract thinking: the use of higher thinking skills to make generalizations, theorize, and conceptualize.

academic freedom: the right of teachers and students to learn, teach, study, read, write, research, and question without censorship or political coercion or restriction.

accountability: the idea that schools or teachers are responsible for educational outcomes and should be evaluated, traditionally through examination of students' test scores.

accreditation: certification that an education program or school has met professional standards.

achievement test: a test of knowledge of or proficiency in something learned or taught; especially a test of the effects of specific instruction or training.

across the curriculum: the theory and practice of teaching essential aspects of one discipline or subject area in other curricular areas, as in "writing across the curriculum," or "reading across the curriculum."

activity curriculum: a curricular approach in which students' active investigations of problems of genuine interest to them take precedence over the study of prescribed subject areas.

adult basic education (ABE): a comprehensive term applied to the education of adults in the areas of primary knowledge, such as literacy, math, social and life skills.

adult literacy: a level of literacy that enables a person in or about to enter the work force to function both as an individual and as a member of society; functional adult literacy.

Adult Performance Level (APL) Study: a comprehensive U.S. national survey of adult coping skills, including reading, writing, computation, problem solving, and interpersonal skills.

advanced placement: courses and programs offered to junior high and high school students to enable them to go beyond the basic required curriculum, often to earn college credit.

advance organizer: an instructional tool using a brief written text before the actual reading of the original text is presented in order to better understand the text. It may be used to suggest connections between the reader and the new material or to help the reader better understand the theme and/or symbolism of a work.

167

affective domain: the psychological field of emotional activity; area of emotions or feelings, attitudes, and values.

age equivalent: a type of derived score based on the age in the test population at which the average person earns a given score.

alternative assessment: authentic assessment; any type of assessment other than standardized testing which measures student performance.

alternative schools: schools that offer a varying approach to education and often offer curriculum and programs aimed at students with special needs.

anecdotal record: a description of behavior; a reporting of observed behavioral incidents.

articulation: the organization of ideas and concepts in a meaningful way; organized into an integrated whole, as an "articulated language arts program."

assessment: the act or process of gathering data in order to determine the strengths and weaknesses of student learning; an evaluation tool designed to measure a student's understanding and ability to apply specific academic skills; also called testing, evaluation, and measurement. Types of assessment (all defined in this glossary) include: alternative or nontraditional, authentic, classroom-based, clinical, content-referenced, curriculum-based, differential, formal, informal, integrated, learner, needs, on demand, and performance.

assessment task: a prompt, question, or scenario to which the students respond.

assisted learning: aided learning; any supportive activity which provides clues or helps a student learn.

at risk: describing a person or group whose prospects for success are marginal or worse.

attention-deficit disorder (ADD): a developmental disorder involving one or more of the basic cognitive processes relating to orienting, focusing, or maintaining attention.

attention-deficit hyperactivity disorder (ADHD): attention-deficit disorder plus hyperactivity; inattention, impulsivity, and deficits in rule-governed behavior, and problems of motivation are characteristic problems of children with ADHD.

authentic assessment: see performance assessment.

back to basics: a movement during the 1980s to revive the emphasis on reading, writing, and arithmetic, advocating fewer electives and more rigorous grading.

basal reading program: a collection of student texts and workbooks, teacher's manuals, and supplemental materials for developmental reading and sometimes writing instruction, used mostly in elementary and middle school.

basic skills: a general term referring primarily to cognitive and language-related skills such as reading, writing, and mathematics.

behavioral objective: a statement of the nature and degree of measurable performance that is expected for a specific instructional outcome, such as setting a goal of writing a short essay without spelling errors.

behavior disorder: disruptive conduct without an organic basis that often interferes with learning or social adjustment.

behavior modification: a technique to change behaviors by systematically rewarding desirable behaviors and either disregarding or punishing undesirable behaviors.

bell curve: a graphic representation of the normal frequency distribution, which shows the average group, usually the largest, in the center or at the peak of the curve; used in education to show the distribution of grades or test scores.

benchmark: translates standards into what the student should understand and be able to do at developmentally appropriate levels; the specific performance or achievement, chosen by goal-setters, that sets the standards for performance.

bilingual education: the use of two languages in part or all of an instructional program, including *transitional* (primary language of the student is used until some level of proficiency in the second language is reached), *maintenance* (the primary language of the student is first used with gradual transition toward the use of the primary language in some subjects and the use of the second language in others), and *immersion* (the second language is used for all instruction in a supportive environment that includes teachers who speak the student's primary language).

brainstorming: open group discussion intended to explore and expand the range of available ideas, to solve a problem, or clarify a concept.

branching program: a kind of programmed instruction or computer program that provides alternate pathways through presented material depending on choices made at each response point, used to adjust to individual differences in interests or learning style or rate.

broad field curriculum: subject areas combined into a new field of study, such as history, geography, and economics combined into social studies.

bulletin board: a surface for displaying messages and graphics, such as a bulletin board for posting artwork; also, a central location in an e-mail network for leaving messages for other computer network users.

career ladder: a system for the career status for teachers of increased pay for increased responsibility and experience.

case history (also, **case study):** a comprehensive, usually narrative report on a student's learning style, behavior, and action taken, along with results and suggestions for further teaching methods and techniques.

ceiling effect: inaccurate measurement of the abilities or knowledge of the most capable students due to inadequate number of test questions.

censorship: refusal to allow access to ideas, whether in printed material, plays, movies, or any other media.

centration: the tendency to pay attention to only one aspect of an event or object.

cerebral dominance: the superiority of one hemisphere of the brain over the other.

certification: state evaluation and approval providing an applicant with a license to teach.

charter schools: public, publicly funded schools that operate much like private schools. Largely independent of their local school districts, they are exempt from most of the rules and regulations that other public schools must follow, such as curriculum decisions, the length of the school day and year, the number of classes students are required to take and what those classes must be, the hiring of faculty, and collective bargaining and tenure. They typically offer innovative programs and are founded by parents, teachers, community groups, businesses, and other organizations after winning the approval of a sponsor, which may be the local school board, a county or state board, or a university.

checklist: a list of specific skills or behaviors to be marked off by the teacher or other observer as the student performs them, particularly for assessment purposes.

child-centered: describing programs in which teaching and learning experiences are selected by the child's own interests and needs; stems from the belief that students develop best when they are free to learn naturally.

child-study team: a group of specialists from various areas cooperating to make a multidisciplinary evaluation of a student's academic and emotional problems.

classroom-based assessment: assessment of a student's achievement based on participation in day-to-day assignments.

clinical assessment: evaluation involving both formal tests and observation of behaviors.

close: to wrap up the day's activities, summarize, to bring closure to a lesson.

cognition: the mental process by which knowledge is gained; recognition, judgment, interpretation, reasoning, and knowing.

cognitive domain: the area of learning that involves knowledge, information, and intellectual skills.

cognitive strategy: a mental approach for problem solution or coping; a way to study.

cognitive style: learning style; an individual's preferred way of learning.

collaborative learning: cooperative learning, learning by working together in small groups.

communication disorder: an acquired or developmental impairment in the ability to send, receive, comprehend, and process verbal and nonverbal symbols.

competency-based education: curriculum that stresses performance and the application of learning to specific tasks.

comprehension strategy: teaching techniques used to help students in their reading strategy, such as previewing the text, linking to prior knowledge, paraphrasing the text, summarizing the text, evaluating ideas, and applying ideas.

comprehensive school: a secondary school with a broad selection of courses in many areas, including academic, vocational, technical, and performing arts.

computer-assisted instruction: a computer program that

aids a student in the learning process by giving step-by-step instructions and options corresponding to the student's responses.

computer-based instruction: teaching that depends primarily on the use of computers.

computer literacy: the knowledge, skills, and ability to operate a computer.

concrete reasoning: thinking characterized by the inability to use abstractions, to plan for the future, to shift mental sets.

conditional knowledge: knowledge that depends on further information or situations.

conference: a meeting or conversation between a teacher and parent or teacher and student discussing student concerns.

constructed response: an essay or short-answer response composed by the student.

content area or content field: a discipline; an organized body of knowledge such as mathematics or social studies.

content-referenced assessment: the use of evaluation items that show knowledge of specific tasks in a content area.

content standards: a compilation of specific statements of what a student would know and be able to do relative to a particular academic area.

content validity: test items that are representative of a specific content area.

convergent thinking: analysis and integration of ideas to reach reasonable conclusions or solutions from available information.

cooperative learning: classroom organization that allows students to work together to achieve individual goals; collaborative learning.

core curriculum: essential subjects required of all students, such as English, mathematics, science, and social studies.

core knowledge: basic skills in reading, writing, arithmetic, and cultural literacy around which a curriculum is built.

core vocabulary: basic words needed to understand a specific field of study or topic.

correlated curriculum: curriculum organized to show the relationship of the content of two or more areas of study.

course outline: syllabus; a brief statement of the goals, objectives, and major assignments of a course, usually listing the dates material is to be covered.

creative thinking: the ability to identify and solve problems in a unique way; divergent thinking.

creative writing: imaginative writing that expresses the writer's thoughts in either poetry or prose, not requiring the accuracy or logic of expository writing.

criteria: the qualities, characteristics, or traits used to evaluate a product or performance.

critical evaluation: judgment of a text or piece of literature by examining its literary features, style, form, content, and purpose.

critical thinking: logical thought process usually connected to the scientific method.

cross-age tutoring: older students helping younger students learn.

cultural bias: knowledge that is dependent on familiarity with a certain area or lifestyle.

cultural literacy: knowledge of important events, values, ideas of a society, familiarity with literature, and historical knowledge of a culture.

culture-fair test: a test that is as free as possible from cultural bias.

cumulative grading: points that accumulate from the first of the grading period to the end, comprising a percentage of the total possible, and then usually converted to a letter grade for reporting purposes.

curriculum: program of instruction; includes the standards and objectives and an outline of how those are to be achieved.

curriculum-based assessment: evaluation of student achievement by using materials and information directly from the curriculum taught.

curriculum guide: a written plan describing the general academic curriculum of a school, school system, or program of study, usually giving the philosophy, specific objectives, and ways of carrying out the curriculum.

curriculum laboratory: resource center, instructional materials support center for teachers.

curriculum validity: a test which shows that the material tested is representative of the curriculum taught.

decentration: the ability to pay attention to several things or events at the same time.

declarative knowledge: factual knowledge a person is able to use.

deductive method: a teaching technique that involves reaching a conclusion and then applying it to specific examples.

deductive reasoning: the act of drawing a conclusion by reasoning from the general to the specific.

desktop publishing: the use of computer programs to assist in the layout and printing of text and graphics.

developmental: reference to behavior relating to growth during one's lifetime; the abilities and skills that are acquired in relation to a point in growth.

developmental age: level of growth as related to age; social age.

developmental lag: developmental imbalance or delay; temporary delay in areas of normal growth.

diagnostic teaching: instruction based on student performance of current tasks.

diagnostic test: a test analyzing strengths and weaknesses of content area skills.

differential assessment: the adaptation of an evaluation tool to the needs of the individual student.

directed reading activity: a reading lesson plan including preparation and motivation for reading, silent reading, vocabulary and skills development, silent or oral rereading, and follow-up or culminating activities.

distance education: education by telecommunication or computers that provides instruction to students who are physically separated from their teachers.

divergent thinking: the generation of new ideas or different interpretations of ideas or information; creative thinking.

domain-referenced measurement: the assessment of learning based on behavior in a specific domain, such as physical education skills.

domain-specific knowledge: knowledge limited to a specific area or influence.

dysfluency: hesitant, faltering, repetitious speech.

dysgraphia: inability to produce handwriting due to brain injury or disease.

dyslexia: a hereditary, developmental reading disability; word blindness.

dysnomia: trouble in remembering words, names, events.

dysorthographia: trouble in spelling due to inability to process language.

early childhood education (ECE): educational programs such as preschool, day care, or nursery school for children before they enter elementary school.

early reader: a child who is able to read before starting school.

educable mentally retarded (EMR): a person, usually with an IQ between 55 and 70, who is able to learn enough to earn a living and have adequate social skills.

education: the changes a person undergoes as a consequence of being taught, either formally or informally; teaching, systematic instruction; knowledge or skill obtained by such a process; the field of study concerned with teaching and learning.

educational measurement: the assessment of schools and their effectiveness in order to improve instruction.

educational media: the materials and means used to instruct, such as television, books, films, videotapes, CD-ROMs, and computers.

educational psychology: the study of educational concerns and methods in order to improve education.

Educational Resources Information Center (ERIC): federally supported agencies in the United States that collect, evaluate, and distribute information related to educational research, theory, and practice.

educational technology: the methods and resources used in teaching; educational media hardware and software as well as the actual design, development, and management of learning processes through instructional systems.

elementary school: grade school, which may include kindergarten through grades 4, 6, or 8; attended by most children usually between the ages of 5 and 12.

e-mail: electronic mail; messages sent and received via computers.

emergent literacy: the beginning stages of connecting print with meaning; the reading and writing behaviors of young children that precede actual literacy.

emergent reading: "pretend reading," early interaction

with printed material that precedes actual attempts to understand print.

empirical validity: validity known by facts obtained by observation or experience.

empowerment: the authority and responsibility of teachers and students to select learning materials, methods of learning, and so on.

empowerment evaluation: assessment by the participants of a study who design, implement, and evaluate a program.

English as a Foreign Language (EFL): a program for teaching English in a non-English-speaking community to students whose first language is not English.

English as a Second Language (ESL): a program for teaching English in an English-speaking community to students whose first language is not English.

enrichment: supplemental activities provided for students that expand knowledge, experience, or skills, replacing review and additional drills.

entering behavior: skills and knowledge needed to begin an activity.

entropy: a measure of randomness or chaos; uncertainty.

environmentalist theory: the belief that the external environment can aid literacy development.

episodic memory: personal memory that is dependent on context.

equivalency test: a test to measure competence, such as the General Educational Development test (GED), considered the equivalent of a high school diploma.

essay: a short attempt in prose to explain the author's opinion or view; a composition.

essay test: a test with questions that call for fairly lengthy written responses, requiring explanation and elaboration.

ethnographic research: the on-site study of classroom teaching; research based on observation.

ethnography: the study of individual cultures; the study of ethnic groups through firsthand observations.

evaluation: judgment of performance; assessment, testing, appraising achievement and growth, including critical evaluation, teacher evaluation, empowerment evaluation, formative evaluation, and summative evaluation.

every-pupil response approach: teaching techniques that require every student to respond to every question, such as signaling, show of hands, demonstrating attentiveness.

examination: test, inquiry, investigation.

existentialism: the belief that individuals are responsible for their own actions; in education, a philosophical stance that provides students with guidelines and information but ultimately the freedom to make their own decisions and experience the resulting consequences.

experience approach: instruction based on student needs and interests rather than on prescribed curriculum.

experiential learning: knowledge gained through experience of everyday life rather than in formal classroom settings.

explicit memory: memory required to recall material to which one has been exposed.

exposition or **expository writing:** writing in clearly organized and developed prose used to explain, describe, or argue.

expression: the act of conveying through words, art, music, or movement; that which communicates.

expressive aphasia: trouble producing sequential, logical, syntactical speech or writing due to brain injury or disease.

expressive language: the use of imaginative, vivid language to convey feelings.

expressive vocabulary: the language needed to express oneself in speech or in writing.

expressive writing: personal writing such as journals, personal essays, diaries, autobiographies, and poetry.

extrinsic method: teaching that includes motivation and rewards from the teacher rather than the student.

flannelboard: a stiff board covered with felt or flannel on which to display pictures, letters, and cut-out figures, used as a visual aid for teaching purposes.

flashcard: cards with numbers, letters, or words written on them, shown briefly to help focus attention and promote recognition of material.

flexible grouping: mixed groups of students rather than ability grouping.

flipchart: a large pad of paper fastened at the top, used to display information one page at a time.

fluency: easy, clear expression.

fluent reader: one who reads easily, smoothly, and with good understanding.

focus: the center of attention or interest; the point of attention.

focused freewriting: writing that is given a time limitation and often an assigned topic.

forced choice item: one of several test answer choices to which one must respond.

formal assessment: standardized test given under controlled conditions.

formative evaluation: the continued assessment of an instructional program by periodically testing the students' progress.

free-response test: an examination allowing the student to answer in his or her own words, such as an essay test.

functional adult education: educational programs for adults emphasizing skills and knowledge used in daily life.

functional literacy: reading and writing knowledge and skills sufficient for everyday life.

fused curriculum: the combination of two or more subjects taught at the same time in one course, such as art, history, and literature in a humanities course.

gateways: specific, required skills and knowledge achieved before moving on to the next level of learning.

General Educational Development (GED) test: a battery of tests given to students who have not graduated from high school, assessing life experiences and knowledge gained outside the classroom, equivalent to skills and knowledge normally acquired in high school.

gifted: possessing special talents, skills, and potential, often indicating the need for special programs or classes, particularly for students possessing superior intellectual, artistic, musical, leadership, or athletic abilities.

global method: a teaching method that emphasizes reading and writing through the use of children's writing, similar to the whole language approach.

grade equivalent: a score based on the grade at which the average student from a standardized test population earns a certain score.

grade level: levels of education in which students are grouped according to age or achievement.

grade point average (GPA): the average of numerical values assigned to letter grades, normally 4=A, 3=B, 2=C, 1=D, used to indicate scholastic achievement.

grammar school: a public elementary school.

grouping: dividing students for instructional purposes, normally by age, ability, or achievement, but to some extent by interest.

group test: a test, such as a standardized test, given to groups rather than to individuals.

gymnasium: a classical school, particularly in Europe, that prepares students for college.

181

handicapped: having a difficulty or disability in performing some task.

Hawthorne effect: an increase in effort because of being motivated by receiving special attention.

Head Start: a federally funded educational program in the United States for low-income children aged four to six, aimed at improving their intellectual, physical, and emotional development and successful readiness for school.

hearing impaired: having any hearing loss.

heterogeneous grouping: the organization of students according to mixed or differing abilities, intelligence, or achievement.

hexter: a six-week grading period.

higher education: education beyond high school; college and university.

higher mental process: complex thinking, abstract thinking.

holistic: referring to the whole rather than to the parts.

holistic approach: teaching that emphasizes the integration of reading, writing, speaking, and listening; providing an overview before teaching the details, then showing how the parts fit the whole; teaching that attempts to help students make connections between the material and themselves.

holistic scoring: the assignment of a single score, rather than scoring individual parts; especially in writing assessment, using criterion-referenced anchor papers for comparison.

homeschooling: the education of students taught at home by parents or someone chosen by the parents, rather than in a public or private school setting.

homogeneous grouping: the organization of students according to similar interests, abilities, intelligence, or achievement.

hyperactivity: excessive or abnormal activity, with easy distractibility and a high frustration level; see attention-deficit hyperactivity disorder.

hypoactivity: less than normal activity; state of inaction, lethargy, or apathy.

illiterate: unable to read and write.

immersion: the total involvement in a subject matter, such as teaching a foreign language by communicating only in that language.

implicit awareness: memory without awareness.

imprinting: learning that takes place in early life through patterning oneself after one's parents or other role model; impression on one's memory.

incidental learning: learning that is not intentionally taught.

inclusion: in education, the placement of students of all abilities in a classroom; mainstreaming.

independent school: a private school.

independent study: an arrangement for a student to work on a project or class on his or her own, usually under the supervision of a teacher.

individualization: adjustment of educational activities to meet the needs of the individual student.

individualized education plan (IEP): a detailed instructional plan designed to meet the specific needs of handicapped students to identify their special education needs, to establish objectives and services, and to design evaluation of their progress; required by law in most states to receive state or federal special education funding.

individually prescribed instruction (IPI): lessons planned for individual students.

individual test: a test designed to test one person at a time rather than in a group setting, usually administered by a trained examiner.

inductive method: a teaching method that examines the details or examples first in order to see common traits and then reach conclusions.

inductive reasoning: reasoning from the part to the whole, from the particular to the general; reaching a conclusion by observing the details.

informal assessment: evaluation by observation or non-standardized procedures.

information: knowledge gained through instruction, study, experience, or research.

information processing: the act of organizing information, either mentally or electronically.

information retrieval: the process of bringing forth information either from human memory, a library, or computers.

in loco parentis: Latin term meaning "in place of the parents"; a teacher or administrator assumes the responsibilities of the parents during the school day.

in-service education: education for employed teachers, offered by a school district, usually taking place over a short period, ranging from a few hours to several days.

instructional framework: the method used to design and analyze teaching.

Instructional Improvement Committee (IIC): a group of teachers from different schools in a district, representing a specific content area or discipline, who meet to work on academic and curricular matters of mutual concern.

instructional media center (IMC): resource center for teachers containing educational materials and equipment, usually located in the library or district media center.

instructional reading level: the reading level that is challenging but not frustrating to students when given normal classroom instructional support.

instructional validity: evidence that test content actually covers curriculum taught.

instrumentation: tests, interviews, surveys, observations, and other means of collecting data to be used in evaluation.

integrated assessment: the holistic evaluation of subject matter-related classroom performances; informal assessment.

integrated curriculum: a curricular approach that reinforces the concepts, skills, and values of various subjects; integrated method.

integrated learning: a method of acquiring knowledge which incorporates several approaches, reinforcing concepts and skills from a variety of areas.

intelligence: skills, abilities needed to process information, general mental ability, capacity to learn, and the ability to think and reason.

intelligence quotient (IQ): the ratio between tested mental age and chronological age multiplied by 100; an index of intellectual potential.

intelligence test: a series of tests for assessing general mental ability or scholastic aptitude.

intentional learning: learning or change in behavior that is deliberate, conscious, and goal oriented.

interactive: having the ability to communicate between persons or between a person and a medium, such as a book or computer.

interdisciplinary: involving two or more fields of study.

interest inventory: a questionnaire or checklist designed to determine one's preferences, interests, and habits.

intermediate grades: in the United States, usually grades 4 through 6.

intermediate school: middle school, grades 5 or 6 through 8.

intern: in education, a student teacher; an advanced student or recent graduate undergoing supervised practical training.

International Literacy Day: September 8, designated in 1990 by the United Nations to recognize the worldwide importance of literacy.

International Phonetic Alphabet (IPA): a standardized set of graphic symbols for transcribing speech sounds in any language.

internship: a specified period of supervised teaching with a master teacher in a school setting during which time an advanced student teacher gains practical teaching experience.

intrinsic method: a teaching method emphasizing that the setting of goals and rewards for learning come from the student rather than the teacher.

jargon: the specialized language of a trade or profession; the special vocabulary peculiar to members of a group; for example, *media center* is educational jargon for *library.*

Job Opportunity and Basic Skills (JOBS): a 1984 report describing job-related skills needed in the workplace in the United States.

journal: a personal record of events, thoughts, ideas, observations, reactions; a collection of student writings; or a periodical published by an association, society, or institution.

junior high school: a school for students in grades 7 through 9.

kindergarten: in the United States, a program or class usually for five-year-olds, conducted as part of the school system or in a private school to prepare young children for the social, physical, and intellectual aspects of school.

kinesics: nonverbal signals used in spoken communication, such as facial expressions, eye contact, hand gestures, body posture.

kinesthesis: the perception of body movement, position, and presence coming from cues within the body's muscles, tendons, and joints.

kinesthetic method: any learning method involving movement.

kinetic learning: learning involving movement.

knowledge: something known; information; learning; familiarity; awareness. Types of knowledge include conditional, declarative, domain specific, prior, procedural, and tacit.

laboratory schools: schools associated with a college or university teacher education program that provide opportunities for student teaching, research, demonstration, and innovation.

lane change: a raise on a salary schedule accumulated by college credits either toward or beyond an advanced degree.

language arts: the curriculum concerned with reading, writing, speaking, and listening; subjects that emphasize the mastery of communication through language.

language center: the areas of the left hemisphere of the brain that are involved in the reception, understanding, and production of language.

language disorder: difficulty in understanding spoken, written, or other symbolic systems of communication, either with the form, content, or function of language.

language experience approach (LEA): a technique that involves student oral dictation to be used to teach reading, writing, speaking, and listening; teaching/learning that emphasizes language experience.

language handicap: a deficiency in the way a person speaks, listens, reads, writes, or signs that impedes communication.

language laboratory: space provided traditionally for teaching a second language, but also for improving one's first language through the use of tape recorders, video recorders, or computers.

language learning: language acquisition; the process of learning to use language; the foundation of developing literacy.

law of effect: the theory that satisfying responses strengthen connections and annoying responses weaken them; used in reinforcement theory and conditioning.

learner assessment: student assessment; testing, evaluation of student learning.

learning: the process or result of change in behavior through experience, instruction, or practice. Types of learning include: assisted, collaborative, cooperative, experiential, incidental, integrated, intentional, language, mastery, perceptual-motor, rote, strategic, and trial-and-error.

learning activity package (LAP): independent learning kit including goals, objectives, directions, materials, activities, and tests.

learning center: a designated area within a classroom especially for specific learning objectives, complete with instructional materials at various learning levels, directions for their use, and self-checking assessments; a center for tutoring and study skill assistance; a learning station.

learning contract: an instructional and often behavioral plan to which a student and teacher agree in order to promote student motivation, self-discipline, and achievement.

learning curve: a graphic representation of performance success in ratio to the number of attempts made or time needed to complete the tasks.

learning disability: any of several disorders in speaking, listening, reading, writing, or computing; students must have discrepancy between expected and actual achievement in one or more aspects of language use to be classified as having a learning disability.

learning hierarchy: the ordering of learning skills from simple tasks to more complex ones.

learning log: a continuing record of learning activities kept by students to help them evaluate and plan their learning.

learning module: an organized group of activities and materials designed to help students reach their goals.

learning rate: the speed at which one learns, often shown as a learning curve on a graph.

learning station: a learning center; a designated area in a media center or classroom.

learning style: a student's preferred way of gaining information, acquiring knowledge or skills, and responding to stimulation; styles include audio, visual, and kinetic.

learning to learn: acquiring skills and behavioral attitudes to make future learning more efficient; learning good study habits that can be transferred to new learning situations.

least restrictive environment: a school learning setting that is the same for all students, including learning-disabled students, in which optimum learning can take place.

left brain: the left cerebral hemisphere, the controlling center for language and calculation functions and for neuro-muscular activity on the right side of the body.

lesson plan: a statement of objectives, organization of procedures and activities, and materials to be used in a daily learning activity.

linear program: a series of small learning steps where students respond and check their accuracy before moving on to the next level of learning.

linguistic reading program: a beginning reading technique based on phonics.

listening center: a designated place where students can listen to recorded instructional material.

listening vocabulary: the number of words a person understands when heard.

literacy: the ability to read; the possession of skills that enable an individual to engage in activities of society, such as reading, writing, and arithmetic; or competence in a special field, such as computer literacy.

literacy fallacy: the mistaken belief that there is a one-to-one correspondence to the written letter and the sound of the letter when spoken, such as the sound of *a*.

literacy gap: the difference between the actual and desired level of literacy.

literacy laboratory: a place where students work on reading and writing skills.

literary merit: an overall judgment of the quality of a literary work, based on factors such as style, characterization, and unity.

literate: able to read and write; acquainted with a field of knowledge.

literate environment: surroundings that encourage reading.

literature-based curriculum: a curriculum that uses literature as the basis for instruction, especially in language arts.

literature circle: a group of students who meet to discuss books they have read outside of class; a book club or book group.

local norms: the test scores within a local community; the range of test scores in a local sample rather than in a national one.

long-term memory: recall that lasts over a number of years, having the ability to pattern and to develop from continued short-term memory, but because of the tendency to distort may not be entirely accurate.

magnet school: a school that offers special program to attract students such as the performing arts, science, or graphic arts.

mainstreaming: the practice of placing special education students in regular public school settings, but not necessarily in regular education classrooms; mandated in the United States in 1975 by federal legislation.

mapping: a planning method for students to explore the connections between ideas or topics, particularly for writing purposes; see mindmapping.

marginalized: a reference to students who are left out of the traditional academic systems, who may or may not be receiving instruction in some other setting besides a school or classroom (hospitals, retention centers, rehabilitation clinics, etc.).

mastery learning: a teaching approach derived from the work of Benjamin Bloom asserting that with clear expectations, most students can achieve a high level of learning if they are given systematic help when needed and if they are given adequate time to accomplish the task; the individual demonstrates mastery of one task before moving to the next.

mastery test: a test of a basic skill that shows whether a certain level of performance can be met or not.

matching test: a test listing answers that must be matched to a corresponding list of items.

matrix: the environment in which something develops, is molded, or embedded.

maturational lag: late development of an individual with no apparent organic defect.

media center: library, or a storage place for educational materials and equipment.

mediation: the resolution or settling of differences and conflict, often by impartial intermediaries.

memory: recollection of past experiences, impressions, recall of information; recognition; or the storage capacity of a computer. Types of human memory include auditory, episodic, explicit, implicit, long-term, short-term, rote, semantic, sensory, state-dependent, and visual.

191

mental ability: intelligence, general intellectual aptitude, intellectual power.

mental age (MA): the chronological age that is average for a given level of performance.

mentally handicapped: mildly or moderately mentally retarded.

mental maturity: adult mental development.

mental retardation: lower mental age than average; a lack of general intellectual ability; *mild* mental retardation—IQ of 50–70; *moderate*—35–55; *severe*—20–40, and *profound*—under 25.

mentor: teacher or counselor; someone who is wise and trusted and gives advice and direction.

merit pay: a salary system based on performance evaluation.

microteaching: short, specific lessons, usually videotaped, used in teacher education for analysis.

middle school: grades 5 or 6 through 8, usually located in a separate facility.

migrant education: classes for students who frequently move from place to place, such as farm workers, usually held during the summer months.

mindmapping: an organizational tool that states the main idea with subordinate ideas branching off and often with descriptions shown on connecting lines.

minilesson: a short teaching demonstration by a student teacher, used for evaluation purposes; a short, concentrated lesson that is part of a larger unit.

minimal brain dysfunction (MBD): a slight brain dysfunction that interferes with learning, but without clear symptoms.

minimum competency survey: a test designed to measure the lowest level of performance in language arts and mathematics acceptable for a high school diploma, also known as minimum competency testing; minimum levels vary from state to state.

mirror writing: backward (mirror-image) writing.

mnemonic: having to do with memory; mnemonic devices are often helpful for improving memory.

model: a standard or example for imitation or comparison.

modeling: serving as a model or example for imitation.

Montessori method: a program of individualized education developed in Italy by Maria Montessori (1870–1952) that emphasizes sensory exploration, responsibility in learning, life skills, and empowerment.

motivation: incentive, inducement, or forces that arouse and direct behavior.

multicultural education: programs and materials that emphasize the similarities and unique aspects of various ethnic groups or cultural groups.

multilevel approach: the use of materials of varying levels of difficulty.

multiple intelligences: sometimes referred to as talents— verbal/linguistic, logical/mathematical, visual/spatial, kinesthetic, musical, interpersonal, and intrapersonal.

multiply handicapped: referring to a person with more than one disability.

multisensory approach: a teaching technique that uses a combination of several senses.

naive processes: practices of beginning readers and writers that are unfocused, often clumsy attempts.

narration: story; an account describing a sequence of events.

narrative chaining: a mnemonic device for recalling facts by relating them in a story.

National Adult Literacy Survey (NALS): a 1992 survey in the United States by the Educational Testing Service of the competencies of adults in reading, writing, and mathematics.

National Assessment of Educational Progress (NAEP): a federally mandated (1969) collection of information regarding the abilities of American students in reading, writing, mathematics, science, history, and geography; "the nation's report card."

National Board for Professional Teaching Standards (NBPTS): an independent, nonprofit organization founded in 1987 made up primarily of classroom teachers, but also including school administrators, local and state school board members, governors and state legislators, education officials, and business and community leaders. They promote National Board Certification, a national voluntary system to assess and certify teachers who meet rigorous standards and to advance education reforms.

National Center on Adult Literacy (NCAL): a U.S. Department of Education literacy center located at the University of Pennsylvania.

National Children's Book Week: a week in November, sponsored by the Children's Book Council, Inc. to celebrate and stimulate children's reading.

National Education Association (NEA): a professional organization of educators, organized at the local, state, and national levels, and concerned with the improvement of education and the working conditions of teachers.

National Institute of Literacy (NIL): a federal U.S. agency for the coordination of literacy projects and reports.

national norms: the range of test scores in a nationwide sample rather than in a local one.

needs assessment: a broad-based examination of goals and objectives in relation to student strengths and weaknesses, perhaps recommending possible changes.

nonreader: a person who fails to learn to read; a person who chooses not to read; one with a severe reading disability; an illiterate.

nonverbal IQ: the IQ score for nonlanguage tasks.

nonverbal test: a test that uses pictures or objects rather than words.

norm: usual or average performance or standard of behavior.

normal: average, within average range.

normal frequency curve: bell curve, particularly one showing the normal frequency distribution of test scores.

normal frequency distribution: the theoretical probability of distribution of scores represented by a bell-shaped curve.

norming population: the groups used to establish test norms or levels of performance.

norm-referenced measurement: the assessment of a student's performance in relation to others in the norming population.

notetaking: a study skill using outlining or summarizing of important ideas in books, lectures, or other instructional sources.

nursery school: a prekindergarten school; a school for preschool-age children.

objective: the purpose of a lesson expressed in a statement.

objectivity: the degree of agreement in test scores when qualified people evaluate the performance, whether it is a behavior or a written test.

object method: the use of objects for observation in order to teach concepts.

official language: a language approved by a government of a country especially for use in governmental affairs, public schools, and business.

on-demand assessment: testing or evaluation done according to the teacher's judgment and time schedule rather than as part of a preestablished process.

open classroom: a large, flexible classroom that may be divided into several areas for instruction taking into consideration group size, space availability, teaching materials, student interests, abilities, and choices, and allowing for ease in movement and simultaneous instruction of the various groups.

open-ended question: a question that is intended to encourage divergent thinking, that requires elaboration rather than one-word responses.

open enrollment: the practice of allowing students to enroll in any school in the school system.

open school: a school with student-centered curriculum, individualized learning, flexible grouping, and open classrooms.

oral reading test: an individual test of oral reading abilities.

oral tradition: stories, legends, and history handed down from generation to generation by the spoken word rather than the written.

oratory: rhetoric; artful, skillful public speaking.

outcome-based education: an educational program using performance assessment for evaluation purposes, measuring behaviors and content taught.

outcomes: behaviors that are the end result of an education curriculum; what a student knows and is able to do after having participated in an instructional program.

out-of-level testing: tests given to students at their level of performance rather than at their grade level.

outreach literacy program: a literacy program offered to participants in an off-campus location that makes it easier and more appealing for them to attend.

ownership: personal investment and control.

paraprofessional: a noncertified aide or layperson who assists educators.

parochial school: a school operated under the auspices of a religious denomination.

pedagese: the complex language found in some articles and speeches in the field of education; excessive education jargon.

pedagogical content knowledge: the teacher's ability to explain how to teach content in his or her subject area.

pedagogy: the art or profession of teaching.

peer response: informal student group discussion of their learning activities.

perceptual-motor learning: learning that depends on non-verbal signals and actually doing or physically performing a function rather than simply being told how to do it, such as learning to type or swim.

performance: action or demonstration of a skill.

performance assessment: measurement using real-life tasks and practical application that requires a student to demonstrate knowledge, achievement, and understanding; sometimes referred to as authentic assessment, demonstration of proficiency, or exhibition.

performance level: the degree of achievement reached by a student on a content standard as revealed through an assessment.

performance standard: a level for judging performance stated in specific criteria.

performance task: a structured situation that requires students to demonstrate their knowledge and skill.

performance test: a test composed of tasks that are actual demonstrations of the student's work; performance assessment.

phonetic: referring to speech sounds.

phonetic spelling: spelling of words according to their pronunciation.

phonics: a technique of teaching reading and spelling that depends on the sounds of letters.

197

plateau: in education, a period of little or no apparent change in performance.

portfolio: a collection of student work accumulated over time to demonstrate the student's knowledge, abilities, and growth toward content standards.

post test: the test given at the end of an instructional period or learning activity.

power test: a test ranging from easy to difficult.

practice effect: any change in performance due to practice.

practicum: the supervised practice of professional skills, usually in the classroom.

predictive validity: the relationship between test scores and later achievement in the classroom or on the job.

prereading: activities designed to prepare for reading, such as background of a story and plot summary.

preschool: school for children from infancy to kindergarten, usually three- and four-year-olds.

pretest: a test given before instruction, a practice test.

prewriting: the stage of writing when a writer finds ideas, does research, and plans the organization of the writing itself.

primary school: elementary school for grades 1, 2, 3 in the United States; ages 5 through 11 in Great Britain; up to 12 or 13 years in Australia.

primer: a beginning book for reading instruction.

print immersion curriculum: a teaching approach that emphasizes a print-rich environment.

prior knowledge: knowledge that comes from previous experience.

private school: a school supported by nonpublic funds and controlled by an individual or group not associated with the government.

proactive inhibition: the interfering effect of information already learned on the later learning of similar material.

probationary teaching period: the time, usually three years in public schools, during which a new teacher must demonstrate competency in order to be granted tenure.

procedural knowledge: "how-to" knowledge.

processing: the activity of incorporating change; the handling of data.

process objective: an educational goal stated in terms of how it is to be reached; for example, *To improve student writing through daily journal entries* is a process objective.

process writing: a writing instruction method that sees writing as an ongoing process including prewriting, drafting, revising, editing, and publishing (sharing the writing with others).

programmed instruction: computer instruction involving step-by-step directions and student responses so that the student can get immediate feedback; computer-assisted instruction.

project method: group learning where students work together on an activity with a purposeful, useful, or worthy goal.

provisional certificate: a probationary certificate, frequently issued to beginning teachers, before all the state requirements for permanent certification have been met.

psychomotor domain: the psychological field of physical activity.

public school: a school supported by tax dollars and controlled by public officials.

publishing: the final step in the writing process, the act of preparing student written material for presentation to an audience, either formally or informally to one's classmates.

pull-out program: a remediation program taking students out of the regular classroom for instruction.

Pygmalion effect: the influence of the teacher's expectations on student performance, as in George Bernard Shaw's *Pygmalion*.

199

random access: the ability to retrieve a specific memory without having to go through all stored information in order.

raw score (X): the number of points earned on a test, before they are converted to a standard scale.

reader response log: a written record of materials read including the reader's reactions.

reader's workshop: a part of a literature-based reading program involving reading, reader responses, and group discussion.

readiness: preparedness to cope with a learning task involving intellectual, motivational, developmental, and experiential factors.

readiness test: a test designed to measure a student's readiness for a new activity or learning level.

reading ability: having the necessary skills to comprehend written material.

reading achievement: the level of reading ability at which an individual functions.

reading center: a place where students get help with reading.

reading clinic: a place where students with severe reading problems receive help from specially trained teachers.

reading difficulty level: the level of comprehension or understanding, usually expressed as a grade level.

reading disability: reading achievement that is significantly lower than that expected for the student's potential and for others the same age with similar cultural and educational experiences.

reading readiness: the potential for benefiting from beginning reading instruction; emergent literacy.

Reading Recovery: an intervention program utilizing trained reading teachers to work with children who, after one year of school, are a reading risk and are in danger of not learning to read at a basic level of competence.

reading specialist: a teacher who has advanced training in teaching reading.

reading vocabulary: the number of words recognized and understood in silent reading.

recall: the act of bringing up in one's memory; types of recall include aided, cued, delayed, free, and immediate.

recency effect: the tendency for events and materials that have been learned recently to be more easily remembered.

reentry program: an educational program for adults who wish to continue their education without having to return to high school.

reinforcement: the strengthening of a behavior, conditioning the probability of repetition.

reluctant reader: one who does not enjoy reading.

remedial reading: special reading instruction for a student reading much below expectancy.

remediation: teaching that attempts to correct a deficiency.

resource center: a library, media center, or instructional materials center.

restructuring: the systemic changes made in a school by teachers, administrators, and parents to make changes ranging from altering the school calendar, school day, and course offerings to the budget, rules, roles, and relationships so that they can serve their community better.

retention curve: performance plotted on a graph in relation to time elapsed since the last learning activity.

retention test: a test given some time after the learning to assess long-term effects.

retroactive inhibition: the interference of later learning on similar learned material; fan effect.

right brain: the right cerebral hemisphere, the controlling center for spatial and nonverbal concepts as well as for neuromuscular activity on the left side of the body.

rote learning: acquiring information or skills by repetition and drill rather than by understanding; rote learning is beneficial in producing automatic psychomotor responses.

rote memory: the exact recall of information learned, often with no understanding.

rubric: a set of criteria that describes levels of performance or understanding. It is used for scoring student work accomplished through a description of the varying levels of achievement on an established scale.

running record: a cumulative account of behaviors.

sabbatical: a leave granted with partial or full pay to a teacher who has taught a specified period of years (often six), to encourage research and professional development.

scaffolding: the instructional method of providing teacher support that can gradually be withdrawn to encourage student autonomy in learning.

school-based management: decision making at the school level rather than by centralized administration; also known as site-based management.

scope and sequence: organization of curriculum to show the levels at which objectives and skills are taught.

score: credits or points earned on a test, assignment, or project.

secondary school: high school, usually grades 9 through 12, sometimes 7 through 12.

self-contained classroom: a classroom where the same teacher teaches all or most of the subjects.

semantics: the study of language and word choice.

semiliterate: able to read and write, but with difficulty; or able to read but not write.

sensorimotor stage: the developmental stage from birth to about two years, during which time intellectual development depends primarily on sensory input and motor activities.

sensory memory: memory gained from the senses.

sequence: the chronological arrangement of subject matter to be taught with attention to difficulty, developmental level, theme, and progression of proficiency.

set: introduction to a lesson, provided to give background, increase motivation, and prepare students to learn.

shared decision making: a management philosophy that involves a broad spectrum of employees, with representation from all of the areas affected, requiring input on most, if not all, decisions.

short-term memory (STM): brief, limited memory, with rapid input and dependent on stimulation for recall.

single-subject curriculum: an instructional program designed around the study of one subject.

site-based management: a management philosophy often used in schools as well as in the private sector, which allows for major decisions regarding budget, curriculum, and day-to-day functions to be made at the site by the people who work there, rather than at a central administration level.

skill: the ability to perform; proficiency; types of skills include basic skills, study skills, and visual-motor skills.

social age: level of growth as related to developmental age.

socioeconomic status (SES): position in society determined by income, education, employment, and social class.

sociology of reading: the study of socioeconomic status, institutions, and family influences on learning to read and reading behavior.

Socratic method: the teaching technique of asking leading questions to help students think rationally and to come up with ideas themselves.

span of attention: the length of time that a person can concentrate on one thing; attention span.

speaking vocabulary: the number of words normally used by a person in spoken communication.

special education: adjusted instruction for students who have different intellectual, emotional, physical, or social needs from the average student.

special needs student: any student who is physically, emotionally, socially, behaviorally, or mentally challenged, disabled, or in need of special instruction, consideration, or attention.

speech and language therapy: the study and correction of speech, language, and voice disorders by a speech and language therapist.

speech disorder: any speech impairment or impediment that interferes with normal oral communication, causes the speaker problems or distress, or calls attention to itself.

speech rehabilitation: speech and language therapy for restoring a lost speech function.

speed reading: accelerated rate of reading; reading that is faster than normal.

sponge activity: any short learning activity, such as a puzzle, word search, riddle, problem, journal response, or individual or group game designed to productively use extra minutes that occasionally occur.

SQ3R: a series of reading study steps: survey, question, read, recite, and review.

standard: a degree or level of achievement, excellence, or attainment.

standard American English: American English as used by most educated sources, institutions, media, and people with social, economic, and political power.

standardization: the establishment of criteria for evaluation.

standardized test: a test with specific procedures to follow, containing identical problems so that the same test can be given in different locations, the norms for which come from many schools and different areas of the country.

standards-based education: a system of instruction focused on student learning of content standards. This system aligns programs of instruction and assessments with the content standards.

Stanford-Binet Intelligence Scale (S-B): an individual test of general mental ability.

state-dependent memory: recall that is better if the person is in a similar emotional or psychological state when remembering as when learning.

steps and lanes: divisions on a salary schedule; steps refer to years in service or experience, and lanes refer to categories determined by degrees earned or credits accumulated beyond a specific degree.

stimulus: anything that arouses activity and causes a response; motivation and incentive.

strategic learning: a learning plan that involves a system to be adapted and monitored.

strategy: a systematic plan to improve learning.

streaming: ability grouping within a class; homogeneous grouping; tracking.

structured overview: a way to organize material to preview, study, and review; a graphic plan that visually demonstrates important concepts.

student journal: a running record of ideas, observations, reactions, and other writings kept by the student and usually read by the teacher.

student teacher: an advanced student of education who gains practical experience in the field by working under the supervision and mentoring of a master teacher.

study guide: specific questions or suggestions to help students learn subject matter content.

study skills: techniques and strategies that help a student organize, interpret, and retain information.

subject: an area of learning and study; discipline; the main idea or topic.

subject-centered: describing a curriculum based on areas of study such as English, math, social studies, and science.

subject matter: a content area of study or field.

summative evaluation: the final evaluation normally including various types of evidence measuring a student's progress or the success of a program.

supplementary materials: materials added to the basic textbooks or program materials required in a course of study, usually for enrichment or extra practice.

survey test: a test to determine knowledge in a broad area.

survival literacy: minimal reading, writing, and mathematical skills needed to function in society.

syllabus: an outline or brief statement of the main units and content of a course of study, usually with some indication of dates or time periods during which work will be covered; course outline.

tacit knowledge: knowledge that one possesses, but of which one is unaware.

teacher center: a professional resource center with instructional materials for teachers to use.

teacher evaluation: the processes used to judge a teacher's professional adequacy; they typically rely heavily on observations and interviews with administrators. The National Board for Professional Teaching Standards (NBPTS) proposes innovative evaluation procedures for the certification of master teachers.

teacher expectation: the attitudes, beliefs, prior experiences, and assumptions with which teachers view individual student performance.

team teaching: an instructional technique involving two or more teachers who plan and teach a lesson or class together.

technical school: a school with emphasis on the skilled trades.

technical writing: writing that communicates specific information in a particular field.

tenure: a system of employment in which teachers, having satisfactorily served a probationary period of teaching, can continue to expect employment.

terminal objective: a statement of specific student behaviors expected based on specific learning activities.

test anxiety: feelings of insecurity and fear when taking a test, ranging from mild nervousness to severe debilitation.

test bias: the differences in test scores between groups that are equal on the material or skills being measured.

test manual: a guide or handbook for the administration, scoring, and interpretation of a particular test.

thematic teaching: the organization of curriculum and instruction around a theme or topic, such as "man's inhumanity to man," rather than around a subject, such as history.

thesis: a formal piece of writing, usually required for an advanced degree, such as a master's or doctoral thesis; dissertation.

thinking: the process of cognition; the producing of ideas, problem solving, including abstract, concrete, convergent, divergent, creative, and critical thinking.

Title I: a federally funded education program designed to serve students of lower socioeconomic status, who are at risk of failure; formerly called Chapter 1.

tracking: the method of placing students in a homogeneous class according to their ability level.

trainable mentally retarded (TMR): those with moderate to severe mental retardation; specifically with an IQ between 25 and 50; they are not usually able to support themselves, but can take care of their own physical and limited social needs and function in a sheltered environment.

transfer: the carryover of skills from one area to another, such as reading skills to writing skills; transfer can be negative, positive, or neutral.

transfer of training: transfer of learning; the recognition of similar learned situations and the application of those learnings to new situations.

treatment: instruction for an individual student based on diagnosed needs.

trial-and-error learning: unsystematic and unplanned attempts at learning; approximation and correction.

unconscious motivation: a motivating force that is obvious to others but not to the learner.

uninterrupted sustained silent reading (USSR): a period of time during the school day when students or everyone in the whole school reads selections of their own choice.

unit: a part of the course, with related materials and activities, taught over a block of time ranging from a few days to several weeks, such as a poetry unit in a literature class.

unit plan: a teaching approach that uses materials and activities from one subject or from several subjects based on a central theme.

validity: the evidence that test results are accurate and that inferences drawn from those results can be trusted.

values: ideals, institutions, customs with which an individual or group identifies; the worth, merit, or usefulness of something.

values clarification: teaching strategies that encourage students to express and clarify their values on a variety of issues.

verbal IQ: the IQ score for language-based tasks.

visual impairment: having partial sight; loss of eyesight due to physical or physiological defect.

visual learning: the acquisition of information through seeing (reading, observing, viewing).

visually handicapped: having serious loss of eyesight.

visual memory: recall or recognition of things seen.

visual memory span: the number of items one can recall (in order) immediately after seeing them.

visual-motor skills: skills requiring visual-motor coordination.

vocational education: a sequence of courses that are directly related to the preparation of individuals in paid and unpaid employment in current or emerging occupations requiring other than a baccalaureate or advanced degree; such courses include competency-based applied learning that contributes to a person's academic knowledge, higher-order reasoning and problem-solving skills, work attitudes, general employability skills, and occupational-specific skills.

volunteer literacy programs: adult basic education programs staffed by adult volunteers.

wait time: the amount of time a teacher waits for a student's response after a question is asked; the amount of time a teacher waits to react to a student's response.

webbing: use of diagrams or maps to show the relationships of ideas; mapping.

Wechsler Intelligence Scale: any of several individually administered IQ tests developed by psychologist David Wechsler that give separate verbal and nonverbal IQ scores as well as a total IQ.

weight: to multiply a score to give it increased importance.

whole language: a professional movement and a teaching belief that all language systems are connected and should not be segmented, but rather taught in context. As much phonics as is needed is taught through writing and the patterns of language in reading with invented spelling encouraged, along with authentic assessment of ongoing student work. Viewed as a natural outgrowth of the way children learn their first language, it is used primarily in the lower grades.

word processing: the use of computers, computer software, and printers to compose and produce text.

word sort: a vocabulary-building activity with words on cards grouped according to categories such as spelling patterns, vowel sounds, and so on.

words per minute (WPM): rate of reading or speaking in terms of the average number of words used in one minute.

word wheel: two concentric circles of cardboard or stiff paper fastened together, each with a series of word elements on it so that when one is aligned with the other, words are created.

writer's workshop: a block of time during the school day devoted to composing, editing, revising, and publishing student work, often with peer collaboration.

writing acquisition: the developmental process of learning to write for purposes of communication, moving from the scribbled drawings of early childhood to the controlled sophistication of the mature writer.

writing center: an instructional area that provides students with tools for writing, editing, and publishing written communication.

writing cycle: the repetition of the writing process until a final product is achieved.

writing portfolio: a collection of student writing accumulated over time to demonstrate knowledge, abilities, and growth for purposes of evaluation and assessment.

writing process: planning, or prewriting, drafting, revising, editing, and publishing or producing a final product.

writing to learn: using writing to help students think about material they have read.

writing vocabulary: the number of different words used in writing.

Young Adult Literacy Survey (YALS): a survey conducted in the United States in 1985 by the National Assessment of Educational Progress, measuring the literacy skills of 21- to 25-year-olds.

young adult literature: books for young adults ages 13 to 18 where the main character is usually, but not always, a teenager; adolescent literature.

zero reject: the principle that no handicapped child may be denied a free and appropriate public education.

zone of proximal development (ZPD): the difference between a child's actual developmental level (measured by independent problem solving) and his or her potential development level (measured by adult-assisted problem solving).

Notable Educators

A quick overview of famous educators who have influenced the direction of public education . . .

MARY MCLEOD BETHUNE (1875–1955). The founder of Bethune-Cookman College and a number of civic and welfare organizations, Bethune is best known for her efforts to educate newly liberated black Americans.

JEROME BRUNER (1915–). Bruner helped establish an American school of cognitive psychology, a movement to study human behavior. He showed that human behavior can be observed, analyzed, and understood in an objective way. He helped legitimize the systematic, objective, and scientific study of human learning and thinking. The author of *The Process of Education,* he argued that more problem solving and direct involvement be used with learners of all ages.

KENNETH CLARK (1914–). The first black appointed to a faculty position at the City College of New York, he wrote *Prejudice and Your Child,* which identified the crippling effects of racism on all children. He fought to desegregate schools and pushed for community action to overcome the educational, psychological, and economic impact of racism.

JOHN DEWEY (1859–1952). Possibly the most influential educator of the twentieth century, Dewey was committed to child-centered education, learning by doing, and the importance of experience. A professor at the University of Chicago and Columbia University, he was also a writer whose ideas helped change education by opening schools and integrating them with the outside world.

HORACE MANN (1796–1859). Mann is best remembered for his efforts to establish free public schools for all Americans and to remove religious instruction from schools. As president of Antioch College, he admitted women and minority students and continued to promote the improvement of the quality of teachers. As a member of the Massachusetts House of Representatives, he denounced corporal punishment, floggings, unsafe buildings, and worked to lengthen school terms, to increase teacher salaries, and to better prepare teachers.

MARIA MONTESSORI (1870–1952). The first female physician in Italy, Montessori was convinced that handicapped and brain-damaged children were capable of much more than most people believed. She established a school called the *Casa dei Bambini* to provide an education for Rome's disadvantaged children. She believed that children need to work at tasks that interest them and if given the right materials and tasks, they will learn best through individual attention. Practical skills and carefully structured sequences of motor skills as well as intellectual skills development are the heart of the approach she advocated, called the Montessori method.

JEAN PIAGET (1896–1980). A Swiss psychologist, Piaget worked with Alfred Binet as he developed the first intelligence test. Through this experience Piaget conceptualized his theory of cognitive or mental development, which still influences the way educators see children: sensorimotor stage: infancy to 2 years (infants explore and learn through their senses); preoperational stage: 2 to 7 years (children begin to understand and organize their environment through language and concepts); concrete operations: 7 to 11 years (they move to more sophisticated concepts such as numbers and processes and relationships); and finally, formal operations, beginning between 11 and 15 and continuing through adulthood (the highest level of mental development — abstract thinking). Piaget's work emphasized the necessity of recognizing a student's mental readiness to learn and relating the learner's needs to appropriate educational activities.

B. F. SKINNER (1904–1990). Skinner's view of human behavior, called behaviorism, laid the foundation for behavior modification and computer-assisted instruction, using the principles of step-by-step instruction, requiring and rewarding student responses. Author of *Walden Two, The Technology of Teaching,* and *Beyond Freedom and Dignity,* his ideas have become quite controversial while providing guiding principles about the technology of learning.

Additional Resources

PROFESSIONAL JOURNALS

American Educator. The Professional Journal of the American Federation of Teachers. Published quarterly by the American Federation of Teachers, AFL-CIO, 555 New Jersey Ave., NW, Washington, DC 20001-2079; telephone (202) 879-4420. Mailed to all AFT teachers, higher education, and other school-related professional members. Subscription for others $8 annually.

Educational Leadership. Journal of the Association for Supervision and Curriculum Development. Published monthly September through May, except bimonthly December/January. Intended primarily for leaders in elementary, middle, and secondary education, but is also for anyone interested in curriculum, instruction, supervision, and leadership in schools. Includes calendar of upcoming annual conferences and professional development opportunities.

Phi Delta Kappan, The Professional Journal for Education. Published September through June, since 1915, for educators at all levels, the *Kappan* is known for its articles and coverage of the important issues in education. Available by subscription to individual educators, schools, and libraries, the *Kappan* covers current issues, trends, and controversies in preschool, elementary, secondary, and higher education. Departments cover federal and state education news, school law, technology, and educational research. Footnoted. Annual index. $35 per year. To subscribe, contact *Phi Delta Kappan*, Subscriptions, Dept. K-AFT, 408 N. Union, P.O. Box 789, Bloomington, IN 47402; to order by phone, call 1-800-766-1156.

REFERENCE BOOKS

Ballare, Antonia and Angelique Lampros. *The Classroom Organizer.* West Nyack, N.Y.: Parker Publishing Co., 1989. With 201 ready to use forms for K-8 teachers and administrators, this collection contains time- and work-savers for every facet of your job, including organizational forms for the classroom, forms for use with students, forms for communicating with parents, and forms for professional growth and development.

Bey, Theresa M. and C. Thomas Holmes, eds. *Mentoring: Contemporary Principles and Issues.* Association of Teacher Educators, 1990 Association Drive, Suite ATE, Reston, VA 22091. A concise publication discussing the realities of mentoring, including suggestions in mentor managing, providing ideas on how to provide support and understanding to the beginning teacher, along with teacher development activities, ways to design training programs and incentives for mentors. Includes excellent bibliography of books and articles dealing with the subject of mentoring. To order, contact the Office of Communication and Publication, Green Street, The University of Georgia, Athens, GA 30602; Phone (404) 542-4592.

Boydston, Joel E. *Teacher Certification Requirements in All Fifty States, How and Where to Get a Teaching Certificate in All Fifty States.* 1994–1995. 12th ed. Paperbound, 164 pp; $20 (includes shipping and handling). Available from Teacher Certification Publications, 603 N.E. Lakeview Dr., Sebring, FL 33870-7008; Phone (941) 382-4795; Fax (941) 382-7136.

Cochran-Smith, M. and S. Lytle. *Inside/Outside: Teacher Research and Knowledge.* New York: Teachers College Press, 1993. 304 pp.; $44.00 cloth, $22.95 paper. This book's purpose is to help practicing teachers, both experienced and novice, understand the value behind their own classroom research.

Directory of Organizations in Education Management, compiled by Stuart C. Smith and Meta S. Bruner. This eclectic guide describes 163 public and private groups devoted to the management of elementary and secondary schools, including publications, services, and top staff. Among them are professional associations, policy research centers, university service bureaus, and school study councils. Paperbound, 70 pp; $8.50 (plus $3 handling charge). Available from Publication Sales, ERIC Clearinghouse on Educational Management, University of Oregon, 1787 Agate St., 5207 University, Eugene, OR 97403-5207; Phone (503) 346-5043.

Directory of State Education Agencies. Council of Chief State School Officers. Thousands of educators and education policy makers are listed here. Paperbound, 113 pp; $25. Available from CCSSO, One Massachusetts Ave., NW, Suite 700, Washington, DC 20001-1431; Phone (202) 408-5505.

Golub, Jeffrey N. *Activities for an Interactive Classroom.* National Council of Teachers of English, 1111 W. Kenyon Road, Urbana, Illinois 61801-1096. Numerous stimulating exercises devised to shift the process of reading and writing from a solitary activity to a group experience; inventive means of communication from the electronic bulletin board to the oral exam; a variety of ways of improving students' performances with language, no matter what class or subject matter they are used in.

Goodlad, John I. *A Place Called School.* New York: McGraw-Hill, 1984. A comprehensive study of schools, teachers and education in America, this large amount of data presents compelling evidence that a thorough revolution of our nation's schools is needed.

————. *Teachers for our Nation's Schools.* San Francisco: Jossey-Bass Publishers, 1990. Presents the results of a massive five-year study of teacher training programs, and addresses the immediate problems of preparation as well as the long-term issues of excellence, while outlining the specific changes that schools of education must make if they are to recruit and develop resourceful and innovative teachers.

————, et al. *The Moral Dimensions of Teaching.* San Francisco: Jossey-Bass Publishers, 1990. Discusses what public schools stand for: the roles, responsibilities, and duties of schools and educators. Based on extensive research, it discusses the interests served in compulsory education for the family, the community, and the individual.

Guide to U.S. Foundations, Their Trustees, Officers, and Donors; and *National Guide to Funding for Elementary and Secondary Education.* Listings for more than 35,000 private, corporate, and community foundations and their key staff, arranged by state and city and by total contributions. Expensive—$195 and $135 respectively. Available from The Foundation Center, 79 Fifth Ave., New York, NY 10003-3076.

Hill, Howard D. *Effective Strategies for Teaching Minority Students*. National Education Service, 1610 W. Third Street, Bloomington, IN 47402. An excellent summary of research and practical data for administrators and teachers of high risk and minority students; the information is timely and useful. Easy to read format. $16.95.

Huber-Bowen, Tonya. *Teaching in the Diverse Classroom: Learner-Centered Activities That Work*. Bloomington: National Educational Service, 1993. Quality learning experiences (teacher-tested classroom activities) are provided, along with a well organized format and exceptional references and resources, to help teachers at every level in every discipline work with all students, especially those in a diverse classroom.

Kuykendall, Crystal. *From Rage to Hope: Strategies for Reclaiming Black & Hispanic Students*. National Educational Service, 1610 W. Third Street, Bloomington, IN 47402. Written by a highly qualified and experienced educator/attorney, this very readable and practical book offers insight and advice in areas such as dealing with differences, self-image, achievement and motivation, obstacles to achievement, discipline, creating a good classroom climate, and strengthening the home/school bond. Each chapter contains an excellent bibliography of related materials.

Lesko, Matthew. *Lesko's Info-Power*. New York: Visible Ink Press, 1996. 3d ed. More than 45,000 free and low-cost sources of information for teachers, students, travelers, artists, consumers, homeowners, job seekers, and more. This book is a treasury of information on all kinds of available resources.

Lowman, Joseph. *Mastering the Techniques of Teaching.* San Francisco: Jossey-Bass Publishers, 1984. Though aimed at college teachers, this book offers an excellent discussion of understanding classroom dynamics, developing interpersonal skills and teaching style, organizing material and leading discussions, as well as making assignments and evaluating student performance. Appropriate for both beginning and experienced teachers.

Mamchak, Susan P., and Steven R. Mamchak. *Teacher's Time Management Survival Kit.* Englewood Cliffs, N.J.: Prentice-Hall, Inc., 1993. Written for new and experienced teachers at all grade levels, this guide contains more than 250 reproducible forms, checklists, letters, and other practical, ready-to-use techniques and time-savers.

Moscovich, Ivan. *Mind Benders: Games of Shape.* New York: Vintage Books, 1986. A collection of intellectual games, learning projects, and puzzles to stimulate creative thinking and problem-solving skills.

Pasch, Marvin, et al. *Teaching as Decision Making.* Longman Publishers, USA, 1995. A valuable resource containing practical strategies for establishing classroom goals, writing instructional objectives and evaluation procedures, designing learning experiences, teaching for individual needs, establishing effective classroom management, and planning for professional growth. Good for teachers of all disciplines at all levels even though it specifies elementary teachers.

Sadker, Myra Pollack, and David Miller Sadker. *Teachers, Schools, and Society.* New York: McGraw-Hill, Inc. 1988. Designed as a textbook for teacher education courses, this book is a virtual encyclopedia of education concepts, issues, trends, and practices. It contains a resource handbook, an update on contemporary issues, a section on student diversity, and is an excellent resource for the most seasoned teachers as well as for newcomers to the field of education.

OTHER RESOURCES

To receive timely top-quality publications, videos, in-service training, and professional development on a variety of topics including:

Discipline with Dignity
Reclaiming Youth at Risk
Cooperative Learning
Thinking Across the Curriculum
Cooperative Management
Parental Involvement

contact National Educational Service at 1-800-733-6786 or (812) 336-7700 or order by Fax at (812) 336-7790. They guarantee complete satisfaction; if you are not completely satisfied with any NES resource, just call within 30 days and they will have UPS pick it up at no cost to you.

On the Internet, of course, there is a whole world of resources and information. Particularly useful to educators specifically are the Academic Assistance Center, Financial Aid/Grant Information, and the Teacher's Network. With all the computer generated information, on-screen animation, and electronic field trip possibilities available to educators, broader, richer content adds to the compelling reasons why everyone should have Internet access. Be sure you visit with your principal, curriculum coordinator, media specialist, or technology coordinator to discover how you can learn more about the Web and integrate the resources of the Internet into your classroom. Dr. Bard Williams (edubard@aol.com) is an educator, writer, and educational technology consultant. He is currently an Education Technology Consultant with Apple Computer, Inc. He is also the author of *The Internet for Teachers* (IDG Worldwide Books), a valuable resource for all teachers.

Television, Technology & Teaching, A Publication of Turner Educational Services, Inc., produced by the makers of CNN Newsroom, is one example of the computer supplemental materials available to the classroom teacher. Subscriptions are free to schools and educators enrolled in CNN Newsroom; others may purchase single copies for $3 each. For subscription information and single copy sales, call 1-800-344-6219.

Index

227